T0146971

An Analysis of

# Milton Friedman's

## Capitalism and Freedom

Sulaiman Hakemy

Published by Macat International Ltd
24:13 Coda Centre, 189 Munster Road, London SW6 6AW.

Distributed exclusively by Routledge
2 Park Square, Milton Park, Abingdon, Oxon OX14 4RN
711 Third Avenue, New York, NY 10017, USA

*Routledge is an imprint of the Taylor & Francis Group, an informa business*

www.macat.com
info@macat.com

*Cataloguing in Publication Data*
A catalogue record for this book is available from the British Library.
Library of Congress Cataloguing-in-Publication Data is available upon request.
Cover illustration: Etienne Gilfillan

ISBN 978-1-912302-22-2 (hardback)
ISBN 978-1-912128-70-9 (paperback)
ISBN 978-1-912281-10-7 (e-book)

**Notice**
The information in this book is designed to orientate readers of the work under analysis,
to elucidate and contextualise its key ideas and themes, and to aid in the development
of critical thinking skills. It is not meant to be used, nor should it be used, as a
substitute for original thinking or in place of original writing or research. References and
notes are provided for informational purposes and their presence does not constitute
endorsement of the information or opinions therein. This book is presented solely for
educational purposes. It is sold on the understanding that the publisher is not engaged
to provide any scholarly advice. The publisher has made every effort to ensure that
this book is accurate and up-to-date, but makes no warranties or representations with
regard to the completeness or reliability of the information it contains. The information
and the opinions provided herein are not guaranteed or warranted to produce particular
results and may not be suitable for students of every ability. The publisher shall not be
liable for any loss, damage or disruption arising from any errors or omissions, or from
the use of this book, including, but not limited to, special, incidental, consequential or
other damages caused, or alleged to have been caused, directly or indirectly, by the
information contained within.

# CONTENTS

## THE MACAT LIBRARY

The Macat Library is a series of unique academic explorations of seminal works in the humanities and social sciences – books and papers that have had a significant and widely recognised impact on their disciplines. It has been created to serve as much more than just a summary of what lies between the covers of a great book. It illuminates and explores the influences on, ideas of, and impact of that book. Our goal is to offer a learning resource that encourages critical thinking and fosters a better, deeper understanding of important ideas.

Each publication is divided into three Sections: Influences, Ideas, and Impact. Each Section has four Modules. These explore every important facet of the work, and the responses to it.

This Section-Module structure makes a Macat Library book easy to use, but it has another important feature. Because each Macat book is written to the same format, it is possible (and encouraged!) to cross-reference multiple Macat books along the same lines of inquiry or research. This allows the reader to open up interesting interdisciplinary pathways.

To further aid your reading, lists of glossary terms and people mentioned are included at the end of this book (these are indicated by an asterisk [*] throughout) – as well as a list of works cited.

Macat has worked with the University of Cambridge to identify the elements of critical thinking and understand the ways in which six different skills combine to enable effective thinking.
Three allow us to fully understand a problem; three more give us the tools to solve it. Together, these six skills make up the **PACIER** model of critical thinking. They are:

**ANALYSIS** – understanding how an argument is built
**EVALUATION** – exploring the strengths and weaknesses of an argument
**INTERPRETATION** – understanding issues of meaning

**CREATIVE THINKING** – coming up with new ideas and fresh connections
**PROBLEM-SOLVING** – producing strong solutions
**REASONING** – creating strong arguments

To find out more, visit **WWW.MACAT.COM.**

# CRITICAL THINKING AND *CAPITALISM AND FREEDOM*

## Primary critical thinking skill: REASONING
## Secondary critical thinking skill: INTERPRETATION

Milton Friedman was arguably the single most influential economist of the 20th-century. His influence, particularly on conservative politics in America and Great Britain, substantially helped – as both supporters and critics agree – to shape the global economy as it is today.

*Capitalism and Freedom* (1962) is a passionate but carefully reasoned summary of Friedman's philosophy of political and economic freedom, and it has become perhaps his most directly influential work. Friedman's argument focuses on the place of economic liberalism in society: in his view, free markets and personal economic freedom are absolutely necessary for true political freedom to exist.

Freedom, for Friedman, is the ultimate good in a society – the marker and aim of true civilisation. And, crucially, he argues, real freedom is rarely aided by government. For Friedman, indeed, "the great advances of civilization, whether in architecture or painting, in science or literature, in industry or agriculture, have never come from centralized government". Instead, he argues, they have always been produced by "minority views" flourishing in a social climate permitting variety and diversity." In successive chapters, Friedman develops a well-structured line of reasoning emerging from this stance – leading him to some surprising conclusions that remain persuasive and influential more than 60 years on.

## ABOUT THE AUTHOR OF THE ORIGINAL WORK

The son of Jewish immigrants from eastern Europe, economist **Milton Friedman** was born in New York City in 1912. He came of age during the Great Depression of the 1930s, an experience that helped shape his outlook for the rest of his life. In 1946, Friedman joined the faculty at the University of Chicago to teach economic theory, and eventually became a leading promoter of its free-market ideas. He advised US President Reagan and British Prime Minister Thatcher in the 1980s, wrote about a wide range of economics issues, and won the 1976 Nobel Prize in Economics for his body of work. He died in 2006 at the age of 94.

## ABOUT THE AUTHOR OF THE ANALYSIS

**Sulaiman Hakemy** holds a master's degree in economic history and development from the London School of Economics. A writer and journalist, he has reported on industry, politics, and culture for various publications. His background is in the development, aid and urban planning sectors, specialising in conflict and fragile states. He is based in Istanbul and Toronto, and speaks English, French, Spanish, Arabic, Persian, and some Urdu.

## ABOUT MACAT

### GREAT WORKS FOR CRITICAL THINKING

Macat is focused on making the ideas of the world's great thinkers accessible and comprehensible to everybody, everywhere, in ways that promote the development of enhanced critical thinking skills.

It works with leading academics from the world's top universities to produce new analyses that focus on the ideas and the impact of the most influential works ever written across a wide variety of academic disciplines. Each of the works that sit at the heart of its growing library is an enduring example of great thinking. But by setting them in context – and looking at the influences that shaped their authors, as well as the responses they provoked – Macat encourages readers to look at these classics and game-changers with fresh eyes. Readers learn to think, engage and challenge their ideas, rather than simply accepting them.

'Macat offers an amazing first-of-its-kind tool for interdisciplinary learning and research. Its focus on works that transformed their disciplines and its rigorous approach, drawing on the world's leading experts and educational institutions, opens up a world-class education to anyone.'

**Andreas Schleicher**
**Director for Education and Skills, Organisation for Economic**
**Co-operation and Development**

'Macat is taking on some of the major challenges in university education … They have drawn together a strong team of active academics who are producing teaching materials that are novel in the breadth of their approach.'

**Prof Lord Broers,**
**former Vice-Chancellor of the University of Cambridge**

'The Macat vision is exceptionally exciting. It focuses upon new modes of learning which analyse and explain seminal texts which have profoundly influenced world thinking and so social and economic development. It promotes the kind of critical thinking which is essential for any society and economy.
This is the learning of the future.'

**Rt Hon Charles Clarke, former UK Secretary of State for Education**

'The Macat analyses provide immediate access to the critical conversation surrounding the books that have shaped their respective discipline, which will make them an invaluable resource to all of those, students and teachers, working in the field.'

**Professor William Tronzo, University of California at San Diego**

# WAYS IN TO THE TEXT

## KEY POINTS

- Milton Friedman was a Nobel Prize*–winning American economist* who was a major advocate of the free market*—that is, a market economy based on supply and demand that does not have a great deal of government control.

- In *Capitalism and Freedom* (1962), Friedman argues for a return to classical liberalism*—a philosophy prioritizing individual liberty above all else—in both economics and politics;* for Friedman, the free market is better than government at catering to people's needs.

- *Capitalism and Freedom* introduced a fresh challenge to the dominance of Keynesian* economics (according to which government intervention in a nation's economy can be valuable); the book's ideas spurred Friedman's rise to fame, and helped shape the American and global economies.

### Who Was Milton Friedman?

Milton Friedman, the author of *Capitalism and Freedom* (1962), was an American economist and public intellectual. He is one of the most influential economists of the twentieth century. An economist is an expert in economics, the social science that studies human behavior and social systems under conditions of scarce means (resources) and unlimited wants.

Friedman was born in 1912 to an impoverished immigrant family in Brooklyn, New York. His interest in economics was inspired early in his life by the work ethic of his parents. He studied mathematics at Rutgers University* and went on to study economics at the University of Chicago* at graduate level. His associates in Chicago subscribed to the emerging Chicago School* of economic thought. The Chicago School opposed Keynesianism, the dominant ideology* (system of beliefs) of the day based on the thought of the British economist John Maynard Keynes.* Keynesianism encouraged governments to intervene in the economy through public policies* designed to achieve full employment and price stability. Chicago School economists discouraged government interference in the free market.

While completing his PhD at Columbia University,* Friedman worked as an economist for the United States government. In 1948, he was appointed professor at the University of Chicago and continued teaching there until 1978. He became a leading thinker in the Chicago School tradition and was known for advancing new ideas on the relationship between the economy's money supply* (that is, the quantity of money circulating) and inflation* (increases in the general level of prices). Friedman argued against Keynesian recommendations for government to stimulate economic growth and lower unemployment by increasing government spending. He argued that this would not lower unemployment. Instead, it would devalue currency and raise prices—that is, it would lead to inflation. Friedman's theory became known as monetarism.*

In the 1970s and 1980s, Friedman became a prominent public intellectual. He influenced a shift in American and British government policy away from Keynesian economics (sometimes referred to as Keynesianism). He was a leading thinker among political conservatives* (those holding political positions in which tradition and free-market economics commonly feature) and libertarians* (that is, those who subscribe to the belief that a government's chief role should be to protect the individual's liberty). In 1976, Friedman won the Nobel Prize in Economics. He died in 2006.

### What Does *Capitalism and Freedom* Say?

*Capitalism and Freedom* was Milton Friedman's first work written for the general public. It deals with the question of what it means to be a liberal—a word with different connotations depending on the context ("social liberalism"* and Friedman's "economic liberalism," for example, are generally understood to describe different political positions). *Capitalism and Freedom* discusses how economic liberals should view the relationship between the economy and politics. The book argues that a free market with minimal government interference is the best way to regulate the affairs of society.

Milton Friedman makes his argument in two parts. The first three chapters lay out the intellectual foundations of the book. Friedman starts by focusing on the term "liberalism."* The original liberals were the seventeenth- and eighteenth-century thinkers of the Enlightenment* (a period that gave rise to a philosophical movement arguing that ideas and behavior should be based on experience, science, and logic, not on tradition and authority). They believed individual liberty was the highest ideal and that it required protection from government tyranny. Later in the nineteenth century, a new generation of liberals softened their stance toward government. They claimed that government plays a key role in enhancing liberty and equality. This point of view became the new "liberalism." The Enlightenment perspective became known as "classical liberalism."

The twentieth-century British economist John Maynard Keynes was a liberal in the new sense. He developed a school of thought called Keynesianism. It taught that by nature markets are unstable, so they need government intervention through regulation or changes in the money supply. By the 1960s, Keynesianism was the most influential school of thought in economics. In *Capitalism and Freedom*, Friedman argues for restoring liberalism to its original definition. He implies that Keynesianism has given too much control over people's lives to the government. For a liberal, government should only enforce the basic rules of society. Anything more begins to encroach on individual freedom.

Friedman argues that economic freedom is a precondition to political freedom. The market*—an economic system characterized by parties making exchanges—is the mechanism through which people live their lives according to their abilities and preferences. These features make the market better than the government at providing for individual needs.

The next 10 chapters of the book discuss these arguments in the context of American public policy (that is, the declared government objectives that affect the whole population). In the third and fifth chapters, Friedman covers government involvement in the money supply and offers his most direct critiques of Keynesianism. He suggests the government should increase the money supply only by a low, consistent amount every year. Additionally, he claims that increases in money supply through government spending (that is, "fiscal stimulus")* make the economy less, not more, stable.

In other chapters, Friedman demonstrates that the market cures social problems better than legislation (that is, better than laws and the enactment of policy). For example, the market is a natural force against discrimination, as discriminating costs money. Also, leaving the education system to the market would increase the quality of education. Friedman also argues for military recruitment through the market and for the end of conscription.* Some of Friedman's proposals are even more ambitious. For example, he suggests replacing complicated tax systems with a simple flat tax*—a single tax rate applied to every taxpayer regardless of income bracket. He also recommends the end of government licensing for professions, including the medical profession.

## Why Does *Capitalism and Freedom* Matter?

*Capitalism and Freedom* presented ideas considered to be on the fringes of economics *when the book was first published*. This was during a long period of Keynesian influence over economic policy. The Great Depression*—the catastrophic economic downturn that lasted from 1929 to the end of the 1930s—was still in recent memory and governments believed that the only way to avoid another downturn was through active intervention.

Despite their fringe status, Friedman's ideas were underwritten by rigorous research by the emerging Chicago School of economics. *Capitalism and Freedom* made these ideas accessible to the general public. It also offered the public the teachings of the Chicago School as an alternative to Keynesianism.

While mainstream academia and the press ignored *Capitalism and Freedom* when it was first published, the book set the stage for a decades-long resurgence of opposition to Keynesianism. It led to later works by Friedman that became influential, and inspired his famous book and television series *Free to Choose* (1980). These works popularized free-market thinking and made Friedman a household name. By the 1980s, *Capitalism and Freedom* had sold half a million copies in 18 languages.

The book foreshadows many of Friedman's later contributions to public policy. Its arguments went on to shape the twentieth-century American and global economies. Friedman's chapters on fiscal policy* (that is, policies concerned with government spending and taxation) led to the development of monetarism, an important school of economic thought focused on the effects of money supply on the economy. His political philosophy spawned the modern libertarian movement. Policymakers drew on his points to remove barriers to free trade and currency exchange.

Academia values *Capitalism and Freedom* much more today than it did in 1962. The book is a seminal text in economics and politics. It introduces students to the ideas of the Chicago School and contemporary classical liberalism. Today, even Milton Friedman's many critics respect his stature in the discipline.

The debate between Milton Friedman and his opponents has resurfaced in recent years thanks to the 2008 Global Financial Crisis* and the European Debt Crisis* (the crisis within the European Union in which several member states have been unable to repay loans to private and public creditors). These are the most significant economic crises since the Great Depression and have created disenchantment with unregulated markets. The market has also been blamed for growing economic inequality. Within economics, the mainstream view is once again slanted to Keynesianism. Yet Friedman's views continue to enjoy wide support among politicians and policymakers. There is not yet a clear consensus on the subject, but the divide has given new relevance to *Capitalism and Freedom* in the public conversation.

# SECTION 1
# INFLUENCES

# MODULE 1
# THE AUTHOR AND THE HISTORICAL CONTEXT

## KEY POINTS

- *Capitalism and Freedom* is one of Milton Friedman's most important works, introducing his worldview to a mainstream audience.

- Friedman was born into a poor immigrant family in Brooklyn in 1912. He became one of the world's most influential free-market* economists* (that is, an opponent of government interference in economic matters), winning the 1976 Nobel Prize in Economics.*

- Friedman's upbringing in a family overcoming poverty* in an economy based on capitalism* (that is, the economic and political system in which production is controlled by private owners for profit) and his work as a government economist influenced his faith in the market* and his skepticism of government.

### Why Read This Text?

*Capitalism and Freedom* (1962) holds a special place in the work of Milton Friedman—a man widely regarded as one of the most important economists of the twentieth century. While the book was not his most commercially successful, or even his most influential within academia, it is a landmark publication.

The book is the first major work in which Friedman, winner of the 1976 Nobel Prize in Economics, introduces his ideas on economics and political philosophy to a mainstream audience. It succinctly encapsulates his perspective in the area of macroeconomics,* the branch of study in economics concerned with the economy as a

> **❝ Humility is the distinguishing virtue of the believer in freedom … ❞**
>
> Milton Friedman, *Capitalism and Freedom*

whole. He developed this perspective during several decades of work as a professional economist, and in the book he develops it further into an ideology* that spans both politics* and economics.

*Capitalism and Freedom* was so far outside of the mainstream at the time of its publication that it is easy to think that Friedman was introducing radical new ideas. One of the most striking features of the book, however, is that it is advocating a forceful revival of existing, but long forgotten, ideas. In *Capitalism and Freedom*, Friedman attempts to redefine the current notion of the political and economic philosophy of liberalism.* He argues for returning the definition of liberalism to its original roots—the classical liberalism* of the period of European cultural history in the late seventeenth century and eighteenth century known as the Enlightenment.* Liberalism, then, was a political philosophy centered on individualism and deep skepticism of government authority.

### Author's Life

Friedman was born in New York in 1912. He came from a poor family of Hungarian Jewish immigrants. His father was a dry goods trader, while his mother worked as a seamstress in a sweatshop,*[1] the kind of factory where working conditions were very poor and workers suffered from long hours and low pay. The family moved to Rahway, New Jersey, when Friedman was one year old. Growing up, he proved to be a gifted student, graduating from Rahway High School in 1928 at the age of 15.[2]

Friedman pursued his undergraduate studies in mathematics at Rutgers University,* graduating in 1932 at a time when the American economy was suffering from the effects of the Great Depression.\* The economic situation inspired Friedman to pursue graduate studies in economics at the University of Chicago,\* which awarded him a scholarship. After completing his graduate studies in a single year, Friedman pursued his PhD at Columbia University\* and simultaneously worked as an economist in various branches of the United States government.

After the publication of his doctoral dissertation in 1946, Friedman gained recognition as a talented economist. He accepted a teaching position at the University of Chicago, where he became a full professor in 1948 and would continue to teach for the next 28 years. During this time, Friedman became one of the most prominent and influential economists in the world. In 1976, the year of his retirement from full-time teaching, Friedman was awarded the Nobel Prize in Economics. He died in 2006, and is now remembered as one of the key thinkers in three main areas of economic study:

- Free-market economics: the economic system characterized by a minimally regulated market for goods and services.
- Political economy:\* the study of the relationship between political and economic forces.
- Libertarianism:\* the political philosophy principally concerned with protecting individual liberty.

## Author's Background

Friedman's perspective as an economist was perhaps most profoundly shaped by the conditions of his upbringing. In a famous interview with the magazine *Playboy* in 1973, Friedman spoke of how his parents' perseverance in the face of poverty reinforced his faith in the market's tendency to reward hard work. His mother, he relates, "worked in a sweatshop … and it was only because there *was* such a sweatshop in which she could get a job that she was able to come to the US."[3] As Friedman puts it, the sweatshop was a "way station" from which workers like his mother eventually moved on, and it was "a far better one than anything available to them in the old country."[4]

Another source of influence in Friedman's life was his professional work as an economist for the United States government. Between 1935 and 1940, the government was hiring economists under President Franklin D. Roosevelt's* New Deal* program. Aimed at combating the effects of the Great Depression, the New Deal was one of the most significant government interventions in the economy in United States history. Friedman began working for the Natural Resources Committee,* which was putting together a countrywide consumer budget survey* (that is, a national survey of average consumer spending). Friedman's experience in this project inspired many of the ideas he would later publish in his landmark work *A Theory of the Consumption Function* (1957).[5] Friedman would later reflect negatively upon the New Deal, which pushed him further toward his skepticism of government interventions in the economy.[6]

## NOTES

1   Eamonn F. Butler, *Milton Friedman: A Concise Guide to the Ideas and Influence of the Free Market Economist* (Petersfield: Harriman House Ltd, 2011), 17.

2   Lanny Ebenstein, *Milton Friedman: A Biography* (London: St. Martin's Griffin, 2009), 5–12.

3   Michael Laurence and Geoffrey Norman, "Milton Friedman: The Playboy Interview," *Playboy*, February 1973.

4   Laurence and Norman, "Milton Friedman."

5   Milton Friedman, *A Theory of the Consumption Function* (Princeton, NJ: Princeton University Press, 1957).

6   Ebenstein, *Milton Friedman*, 35.

# ACADEMIC CONTEXT

## KEY POINTS

- Economics* is the study of human behavior and social systems under conditions of scarce means (resources) and unlimited wants.

- In the mid-twentieth century economics was characterized by a strong preference for Keynesianism*—the position that government could intervene in the economy in the interests of prosperity.

- Milton Friedman was influenced by the Austrian School* of economic thought (according to which the rationality and action of the individual is of chief importance), and by his colleagues in the Chicago School* of economic thought (according to which the market* should be allowed to operate without hindrance).

### The Work in its Context

Had Milton Friedman's *Capitalism and Freedom* been published just three decades earlier, it would have received a warm academic welcome; in the decades prior to the publication of the British economist John Maynard Keynes's* *The General Theory of Employment, Interest, and Money* in 1936,[1] economic thought in the English-speaking world "was completely dominated by free-market* orthodoxy"[2]—the belief in an economic system based on supply and demand and characterized by little or no government control.

However, by the time *Capitalism and Freedom* was published in 1962, mainstream economists viewed Friedman's ideas as "fringe notions."[3] The crises of the economic downturn known as the Great Depression* and World War II* (1939–45) had attracted economists

> ❝ Those of us who were deeply concerned about the danger to freedom ... from the triumph of the welfare state and Keynesian ideas, were a small beleaguered minority regarded as eccentrics ... ❞
>
> Milton Friedman, *Capitalism and Freedom*

and policymakers to Keynes's teachings. Keynes had justified government intervention into the economy as a way of stabilizing sometimes erratic forces. This thinking was reflected in crisis-era economic policymaking in the 1930s and 1940s, and it continued to dominate the political landscapes of Western countries into the early 1960s.

*Capitalism and Freedom* represented the first, and most important, step in the resurgence of the free-market principles that had been so influential before their rapid erosion by the rise of Keynes. The publication of *Capitalism and Freedom* set the stage for a debate that would define the discipline of economics throughout the second half of the twentieth century and even today.

### Overview of the Field

In the mid-twentieth century English-speaking world, the field of economics was characterized primarily by two camps: Keynesianism, which encourages government intervention in the economy through public policies,\* and free-market economics, a system in which prices are determined by competition between privately owned businesses unrestricted by government. Keynesianism was the dominant force at the time that *Capitalism and Freedom* was written, and it is also the school of thought that Friedman argues against in his book.

John Maynard Keynes, for whom the Keynesian school of thought is named, rose to prominence for challenging the laissez-faire\* policies that had characterized Britain and, to a great extent, America prior to the Great Depression. Laissez-faire economics minimized government involvement in economic affairs and maintained that the forces of the free market—that is, the supply and demand of goods and services—would automatically generate appropriate prices and full employment. Keynes's work demonstrated that prices and wages were usually slow to respond to the forces of supply and demand, and that demand was a more important force in driving economic growth. In other words, markets themselves were fundamentally inefficient and prone to "boom and bust"* cycles based on changing demand. Boom and bust cycles are a characteristic of capitalist* economic systems in which the economy passes between dramatic phases of expansion and contraction. Keynes's proposed solution to these problems was increased government spending and intervention in the economy, primarily to stimulate demand.

Free-market economists were divided into two schools of thought: the Austrian School and the Chicago School. Both were united by a shared support for private enterprise* (that is, for-profit businesses owned by private individuals or corporations), low taxes, minimal government, and preserving the value of an economy's money supply.* Their differences were largely born of historical events and disagreements in methodology. The Austrian School, whose adherents included Keynes's rival, the Austrian British economist Friedrich von Hayek,* predated Keynesianism and minimized the use of quantitative analysis* to back theory. Quantitative analysis is a way of understanding behavior by using complex mathematical and statistical modeling and research. In contrast, the Chicago School, in which Friedman was a leading thinker, formed in the 1950s and placed great emphasis on quantitative analysis. The Chicago School eventually became the more influential of the two, and this is the main reason that the study of economics is considered a quantitative science today.

## Academic Influences

As with other classical liberal* economists, the original influence for Friedman's economic views was the work of the eighteenth-century political economist Adam Smith.* Smith famously coined the term "the invisible hand"[4] to describe the ability of free-market forces to create desirable outcomes for the population. Smith's assertions that the free market exists and is the most efficient way to meet people's needs laid the foundation upon which classical economics is based.

Friedrich von Hayek of the Austrian School provided a more immediate intellectual backdrop for Friedman's ideas. Hayek's book *The Road to Serfdom* (1944), according to Friedman, "was really an amazing event when it came out."[5] Early in his career, Friedman attended a series of meetings hosted by Hayek in Switzerland for the Mont Pelerin Society,* an international discussion group concerned with furthering understanding of political and economic freedom. At these meetings, Friedman and Hayek "were fostering essentially the same set of ideas,"[6] and this similarity would eventually grow to the point where Friedman became the group's leader after Hayek's retirement. This is one of the reasons Friedman is seen as Hayek's successor as the face of twentieth-century free-market economics, even though the two had many intellectual disagreements.

Friedman's other great influences were his academic mentors. These included Arthur Burns,* who was Friedman's professor at Rutgers University* and who later served as chairman of the United States Federal Reserve* (the central bank of the United States). The original leaders of the Chicago School, Jacob Viner,* Frank Knight,* and Henry Simons,* were economists and teachers at the University of Chicago;* they "played a major influence in shaping [Friedman's] attitudes and views"[7] during his graduate school studies.

## NOTES

1   John Maynard Keynes, *The General Theory of Employment, Interest, and Money* (London: Palgrave Macmillan, 1936).

2   Paul Krugman, "Who Was Milton Friedman?" *New York Review of Books*, February 15, 2007.

3   Greg Ip and Mark Whitehouse, "How Milton Friedman Challenged Economics, Policy and Markets," *Wall Street Journal*, November 17, 2006, accessed January 5, 2016, http://www.wsj.com/articles/SB116369744597625238.

4   Adam Smith, *The Theory of Moral Sentiments* (London: A. Millar, 1759), 350.

5   Milton Friedman, interview by Brian Lamb, *Milton Friedman: 50th Anniversary Edition of F. A. Hayek's Road to Serfdom*, C-SPAN Booknotes, November 20, 1994, accessed March 24, 2016, http://www.c-span.org/video/?61272-1/book-discussion-road-serfdom

6   Friedman, interview by Lamb.

7   Friedman, interview by Lamb.

# MODULE 3
# THE PROBLEM

## KEY POINTS

- In the field of economics,* Keynesians,* who advocated a mixture of free-market* policies and government intervention, came to dominate academia and public policy.*

- When Milton Friedman's *Capitalism and Freedom* was published, true liberals* (that is, free-market economists) were divided and on the fringes of economics—in the nineteenth and early twentieth centuries, the liberal identity had been claimed by many economists and political* philosophers who had forsaken its original emphasis on individualism and distrust of government.

- *Capitalism and Freedom* is an attempt to restore the definition of liberalism* to its original sense and to place economics at the heart of it.

### Core Question

While Milton Friedman's *Capitalism and Freedom* argues for a classical liberal* worldview, at its heart the book is concerned with the core question of what it means—philosophically, politically, and economically—to be a liberal. This gives the focus of the book a reach extending far beyond economics. But it still takes economics as its primary concern because it argues that, under Friedman's definition of liberalism, the liberal ought to consider economic freedom as a precondition for political freedom.

While all liberals in the mid-twentieth century found their original inspiration in the ideas set out by the foundational British economist Adam Smith* in his book *The Wealth of Nations* (1776), the

> ❝ As liberals, we take freedom of the individual, or perhaps the family, as our ultimate goal in judging social arrangements. ❞
>
> Milton Friedman, *Capitalism and Freedom*

disagreements that occurred throughout the nineteenth and twentieth centuries between economists and political theorists within their own disciplines led to a crisis of identity and definition over what the term "liberal" means. John Maynard Keynes\* and Friedrich von Hayek,\* the two archrivals who set the stage for the publication of *Capitalism and Freedom*, were both ideological liberals. That is, they both believed in individual liberty and equality and shared "a distaste for authoritarian regimes such as communism\* and fascism\*"[1] (communism is a social and political system in which common ownership of the tools and resources required for production is considered a means to abolish social hierarchy; fascism is a political system founded on fierce notions of nationhood and intrusive government control). Keynes's beliefs, however, were more tempered. He argued that some government intervention was necessary in order to preserve the integrity of the economy. Von Hayek, Friedman's immediate intellectual predecessor, was more extreme in his views, arguing that "any increase in state planning is the first step on the way to tyranny."[2]

Friedman's concern in *Capitalism and Freedom* is to reclaim von Hayek's position, but to elaborate upon it and adapt it to suit some of his own economic theories. The book re-empowers an older interpretation of liberalism that is totally skeptical of the state as the enabler of individual freedom, and lays out a detailed policy platform for "true" liberals to support.

### The Participants
The split in liberalism evolved over the course of history as new participants took up the ideology.\* The original form of liberalism, or

"classical liberalism" as it became known, was formulated by the philosophers of the Enlightenment,* who emphasized liberty, equality, and reason. British philosophers Thomas Hobbes* and John Locke* reasoned in the seventeenth century that individual human beings had natural rights and freedoms, which could only be guaranteed against tyranny through a social contract between the public and its government. This thinking spread in the eighteenth century to the United States with political thinkers like Thomas Paine,* who wrote in his pamphlet *Common Sense* (1776) that "government even in its best state is but a necessary evil."[3]

By the nineteenth century, however, a new generation of liberal philosophers had softened the ideology's stance toward government. These thinkers, including the British political philosophers Thomas Hill Green* and John Hobson,* argued that the state had a duty to actively promote and enhance individual freedom, which involved the character of society as much as the motivations of individuals.

Although John Maynard Keynes was brought up a classical liberal, the economic crises associated with the Great Depression* and World War II* eventually instilled in him an appreciation for social welfare policies and other forms of government interventionism. From the publication of his *General Theory of Employment, Interest, and Money* in 1936 until the resurgence of classical liberalism in the 1960s and 1970s, Keynes's influence meant that, within the discipline of economics, liberals could promote the primacy of capitalism* and the market*— but still allow for both of those things to be supported by the intervention of government.

### The Contemporary Debate

Milton Friedman's publication of *Capitalism and Freedom* was an attempt to reintroduce a debate within economics that had all but died down in the early 1960s. While the field of economics was divided into Keynesianism and free-market economics, the lion's share of economists subscribed to the former. John Maynard Keynes earned his fame 30 years earlier, and the success of his teachings was sustained by two economic events that shook the Western World: the Great Depression and the start of World War II. Both of these events required large-scale government intervention in the economy to an extent that permanently stifled any talk of laissez-faire* economic policies.

Free-market economists within the Austrian School* (for whom economic analysis began with assumptions regarding the rational nature of the individual's economic behavior) and, after the 1950s, the Chicago School* (for whom the market should be allowed to operate without hindrance) continued to engage in economics research from an anti-Keynesian perspective, even though their contributions to the discipline were overshadowed by a preference for Keynesian economics in academia and policy. But while the Austrian and Chicago Schools of thought had much in common, an intense debate raged between them over methodological issues. The Austrian School, which included Keynes's archrival Friedrich von Hayek,* minimized the use of quantitative analysis.* But Friedman's own Chicago School placed more emphasis on this type of analysis.

## NOTES

1   *Economist*, "Keynes and Hayek: Prophets for Today," March 14, 2014, accessed January 5, 2016, http://www.economist.com/blogs/freeexchange/2014/03/keynes-and-hayek.

2   *Economist*, "Keynes and Hayek."

3   Thomas Paine, *Common Sense* (Philadelphia: R. Bell, 1776), 69.

# THE AUTHOR'S CONTRIBUTION

## KEY POINTS

- Milton Friedman's *Capitalism and Freedom* redefines liberalism\* and demonstrates that, for the liberal, economic\* freedom is a precondition for political\* freedom.

- *Capitalism and Freedom* hugely strengthened support for a new liberal school of thought in twentieth-century economics.

- At the time of its publication, *Capitalism and Freedom* represented the official answer of the Chicago School\* of economic thought—to which Friedman subscribed—to the ideas of Keynesianism.\* It also helped to popularize the beliefs of the Chicago School, bringing them to a broader audience.

### Author's Aims

Milton Friedman has two overarching aims in *Capitalism and Freedom*. The first is a broad aim, which is to reposition the liberal worldview firmly within the camp of classical liberalism\* and its intellectual descendants in the Austrian School\* and Chicago School traditions of economics. To do so would require redefining liberalism and extricating it from the dominant assumptions and analytical methods of the 1950s, which favored a Keynesian balance between individual freedom and government intervention. Friedman devotes the first two chapters of his book to establishing the arguments related to this aim.

After establishing the central position of freedom in the liberal worldview, Friedman's second aim is to build a case for the necessity of economic freedom as a precondition for political freedom. The two

> ❝ Attempting to portray the work of Milton Friedman ...
> is like trying to catch the Niagara Falls in a pint pot. ❞
> John Burton, *Twelve Contemporary Economists*

are framed in *Capitalism and Freedom* as inseparable, though it is clear from the book's arguments that economic freedom is more urgent. Friedman's case is built on the idea that control over affairs should to be handed over to individuals to the greatest extent possible. Friedman aims to demonstrate the superiority of individual control over government control across a wide range of public policy* issues—he shows that this superiority is usually achieved through the market,* which coordinates individual interests with minimal interference from top-down authority.

### Approach

Friedman's introductory chapter lays the foundation for the rest of the book, but most importantly it elaborates in detail upon the idea of liberalism. Friedman fulfills the first of his two aims in this chapter, tracing the origins of liberalism to the Enlightenment* thinkers of the eighteenth century. He reconstructs the original idea of liberalism, reminding the reader that the mainstream definition of liberalism in the mid-twentieth century (the time of the book's publication) is a distortion of the concept. This establishes the conceptual framework in which the book's arguments will be made. The first and second chapters elaborate upon this conceptual framework, establishing a link for the reader between economic and political freedom, from the liberal perspective.

Another important element of Friedman's approach in *Capitalism and Freedom* is the diverse evidence base that he employs. Chapters 3 to 12 are built around detailed discussions of public policy, illustrating Friedman's use of real-life social, political, and economic problems in the United States to give the reader an idea of how real liberalism might be put into practice. Connected to these discussions, however, are Friedman's frequent references to political philosophy and the history of economic thought. Overall, Friedman uses history, philosophy, and empirical analysis—analysis based on evidence verifiable by observation—to construct his case.

## Contribution in Context

*Capitalism and Freedom* was the most comprehensive refutation of John Maynard Keynes's* notion of economic liberalism written for a mainstream audience. This is the source of its eventual popularity and success. The book is also the embodiment of what the Chicago School stood for under Friedman's intellectual stewardship. As such, it can be read as the Chicago School's official answer to the dominance of Keynesianism in the economics discourse.

Beyond its refutation of Keynesianism, *Capitalism and Freedom* can also be viewed as a significant contributor to the Chicago School's eventual success as an academic tradition. The Chicago School was more focused on quantitative analysis than its closest competitor, the Austrian School, which had produced many polemics* (that is, pieces of writing that directly attack an opinion or theory, and that are intended to persuade readers of the writer's point of view) for a broad audience. Friedrich von Hayek's* *The Road to Serfdom* (1944), for example, was the dominant anti-Keynesian work of the time. In some ways, *Capitalism and Freedom* played an important role in making the ideas of the Chicago School more accessible to those without mathematical training, just as *The Road to Serfdom* had done for the Austrian School.

The final contribution that *Capitalism and Freedom* makes is in its application of classical liberal ideas to the contemporary context of the United States. The central beliefs of liberalism that Friedman invokes were first conceived when the United States was in its very earliest stages of development. For most Americans in 1962, these ideas were so far in the past that they were seen more as academic concepts than as anything applicable to political debates that were taking place at that time. But what *Capitalism and Freedom* achieves is to address the major public policy issues of its time head-on. And with its reinterpretation of classical liberalism, it offers us a long-forgotten, but pertinent, perspective on the nature of our engagement with government and society.

# SECTION 2
## IDEAS

# MAIN IDEAS

## KEY POINTS

- *Capitalism and Freedom*'s major themes are liberalism\* and the superiority of the market\* (that is, the social and economic system of capitalism)\* over government as a way of mediating the affairs of individuals.

- Milton Friedman argues that, for liberals, economic freedom is integral to the existence of political freedom; furthermore, economic freedom can only be ensured through the market.

- While Friedman's writing in *Capitalism and Freedom* deals with abstract, academic concepts, it is ultimately accessible to a broad audience.

### Key Themes

The driving ideological forces behind *Capitalism and Freedom* are Milton Friedman's own view of liberalism, from which his understanding of economic and political freedom is derived, and his belief in the primacy of the market over government as a means of resolving the affairs of society. Put another way, the two major themes of the book are, first, the implications of Friedman's idea of liberalism and, second, the primacy of the market over government.

For Friedman, these two themes are linked, as any liberal should view the market as the best instrument for regulating affairs in society. Friedman reinforces this link by introducing both ideas together in the first three chapters of his book. His introductory chapter lays the ideological groundwork for this link, and the first two numbered chapters illustrate it. In the ten chapters that follow, he continues to employ his two key themes as frameworks for discussion rather than as

> **❝** Underlying most arguments against the free market is a lack of belief in freedom itself. **❞**
>
> Milton Friedman, *Capitalism and Freedom*

sole arguments. Consequently, the liberal notion of freedom and a strong preference for the market are ideas that run as linked undercurrents throughout the book.

### Exploring the Ideas

*Capitalism and Freedom* was published at a time when Keynesianism* had evolved the notion of liberalism into something based on a political compromise between the individual and society. Friedman laments this "corruption of the term liberalism" because he feels its meaning has been shifted away from its eighteenth-century classical liberal* origins, which allow for little government involvement in the affairs of individuals, including economic affairs.[1] In the introductory chapter of *Capitalism and Freedom*, Friedman describes the twentieth-century liberal as someone who "in the name of welfare and equality … has come to favor a revival of the very policies of state intervention and paternalism* against which classical liberals fought"[2] ("paternalism" here denoting the restriction of the individual's freedom by the forces of authority in the name of his or her own best interests). He then echoes the sentiments of the Austrian American economist* Joseph Schumpeter* on the state of liberalism: "the enemies of the system of private enterprise* have thought it wise to appropriate this label."[3]

Friedman does not call for the total absence of government. Liberalism in its true form, he writes, calls for laissez-faire* economics at home, free trade* (that is, unhindered exchange of goods and services) abroad, and "the development of representative government … reduction in the arbitrary power of the state, and protection of the civil freedoms of individuals."[4] Friedman is clear that the liberal should desire a government, but one that reaches no further than the minimum amount required from it.

The first two chapters of *Capitalism and Freedom* are concerned with establishing the correct relationship between politics* and the economy from the liberal perspective. Friedman frames the relationship in terms of freedom, which is the overarching concern of the liberal. Economic freedom, Friedman argues, is the precondition for political freedom, giving the former a more immediate urgency.

In the first chapter, "The Relation between Economic Freedom and Political Freedom," Friedman aims to resolve the tension between the need for individuals to be free and the need for their economic relations with one another to be coordinated. He argues that while government is essential to determine the "rules of the game" and to enforce those rules, "the fundamental threat to freedom is power to coerce, be it in the hands of a monarch, a dictator, an oligarchy* [a small elite], or a momentary majority."[5] In other words, government will always pose a potential danger to liberty.

It is crucial, in Friedman's view, for the liberal to separate the economy from political control in order for "economic strength to be a check to political power rather than a reinforcement."[6] Friedman's second chapter elaborates upon and strengthens this argument. The end result is that Friedman restores the definition of liberalism to its classical sense, which involves a deep skepticism of government, and positions the economy as the frontline in which liberals must fight for their values.

The economic frontline is where Friedman spends most of his energy in *Capitalism and Freedom*. Most of the remaining chapters are devoted to different economic issues including trade, fiscal policy,* education, discrimination, monopoly* (a state in which a single individual or body is the sole supplier of something that might be purchased), occupational licensure* (that is, a system of government-recognized licenses to practice given professions), income distribution* (the division of a nation's wealth between its citizens), welfare (state-mandated protections for a nation's most economically vulnerable citizens), and poverty.* Friedman analyzes each of these issues in detail, building a case for the superiority of the market and the inability of government intervention to provide positive outcomes.

## Language and Expression

*Capitalism and Freedom*'s language and expression are born of Milton Friedman's own life experience and perspectives. Friedman is an economist, a critic of government, a capitalist, and a liberal in the classical sense. He approaches his subject matter academically, though when it comes to his key points he simplifies his language enough to appeal to a broader audience.

Friedman is first and foremost an economist. This is why the content of entire chapters of his book deals with complex and technical economic subjects such as fiscal policy or free-floating exchange rates* (that is, currency regulation in which the nominal values of currencies are allowed to fluctuate with market conditions). He even devotes an entire chapter to occupational licensure, which, while neither complex nor technical, would seem mundane to those outside of academia. But Friedman does relegate the more tedious research behind some of his claims to citations of past studies or articles for interested readers to pursue in their own time.

The overall tone of the book is a balance between the optimism and cynicism found in liberal thinking, and this is what makes the book engaging to the average reader. Friedman's writing on the power of markets to prompt creativity is upbeat, while his criticisms of both socialism* (the political ideology* advocating social or democratic control over an economy's resources) and government intervention are scathing. In *Capitalism and Freedom*, Friedman does not employ the negative language and expression of a critic, but rather puts across the consideration of an educated, but passionate, subscriber to an ideology.

## NOTES

1  Milton Friedman, *Capitalism and Freedom* (London: University of Chicago Press, 1962), 6.

2  Friedman, *Capitalism and Freedom*, 5.

3  Friedman, *Capitalism and Freedom*, 5.

4  Friedman, *Capitalism and Freedom*, 5.

5  Friedman, *Capitalism and Freedom*, 15.

6  Friedman, *Capitalism and Freedom*, 15.

# MODULE 6
# SECONDARY IDEAS

## KEY POINTS

- Two important ideas throughout *Capitalism and Freedom* are the vulnerable nature of freedom and that any concentration of power, no matter how well meaning, is prone to cause harm.

- *Capitalism and Freedom*'s secondary themes went on to inspire the modern libertarian* movement.

- In *Capitalism and Freedom*, Milton Friedman introduces some of his ideas about monetarism,* though they gained prominence in his later work.


### Other Ideas

In addition to the notions of liberalism* and the primacy of the market,* Milton Friedman also uses *Capitalism and Freedom* to illustrate ideas relating to freedom and the concentration of power. These are found within the book's key themes; the most significant among them is that freedom itself is a vulnerable, fragile concept. Although this idea is linked to *Capitalism and Freedom*'s key themes, it is ultimately distinct from them. The vulnerable nature of freedom is the backdrop to Friedman's arguments for the primacy of the market, and he also uses it to go deeper into the psychology of classical liberalism.*

Another idea Friedman draws upon is the ineffectiveness of authority in regulating the individual's affairs. This is a separate idea from his distrust of government's intention, and from his idea concerning the freedom offered by the marketplace. For Friedman, even a benevolent and well-meaning government is a potentially dangerous one. This is important to understand in order to more

> 66 Nothing is so permanent as a temporary
> government program. 99
> Milton Friedman, *Tyranny of the Status Quo*

accurately interpret Friedman's attitude toward government. It is often thought that Friedman is completely hostile to government because it supposedly harbors tyrannical motives. The reality is more nuanced; Friedman does not see all government as the enemy of freedom. More often, he views it as a liability to freedom.

### Exploring the Ideas

Throughout *Capitalism and Freedom*, it is clear that Milton Friedman, in the classical liberal tradition, values individual freedom above all else. This can create an impression for readers of freedom as an ideological\* force. However, the book provides considerable insight into how the author actually views the nature of freedom. Friedman discusses this most prominently in the introductory and concluding chapters of his book. To him, freedom is not an ideology as strong as any other that must contend with its opponents on an equal footing. In the book's opening pages, Friedman writes, "freedom is a rare and delicate plant."[1]

The fragile nature of freedom is precisely why Friedman makes an argument that at first seems contradictory to his aims, but is ultimately reasoned: the existence of government is a necessity, but only for the very specific and limited task of protecting the existence of freedom. Furthermore, Friedman shows that while classical liberals such as himself consider freedom to be a natural right for human beings, it is not their natural condition. Throughout history, large parts of the world have never known freedom in the liberal sense. "The typical state of mankind," Friedman writes, "is tyranny, servitude, and misery."[2] What little freedom exists, Friedman attributes to the period of European cultural history known as the Enlightenment* and the subsequent influence of liberals in the Western world.

While government must exist to ensure freedom's preservation, Friedman ultimately views authority in general, and especially authority in the form of government, as being prone to tragedy. Even a benevolent authority can inflict disaster upon a population if its control over society is allowed to increase too much. Throughout *Capitalism and Freedom*, Friedman cites a series of examples in which the United States government adopts well-meaning policies that turn out to be inefficient and threatening to freedom.

These include: interference with prices and foreign trade that intends to protect jobs but raises prices for consumers and jeopardizes international relations; mandating licenses for medical workers that are meant to ensure a minimum quality but make healthcare unaffordable and encourage the use of black-market alternatives; and a government-legislated minimum wage* that, while designed to ensure a minimum standard of living, forces employers to cut the number of available jobs. To Friedman, all of these examples show that the government does not need to be hostile in order to damage the lives of individual citizens, or even society as a whole. In his concluding chapter, Friedman writes, "Concentrated power is not rendered harmless by the intentions of those who create it."[3]

### Overlooked

One of *Capitalism and Freedom*'s most overlooked aspects is Friedman's views on the relationship between an economy's money supply* (the quantity of money circulating in the economy) and inflation* (the increase in the general level of prices in an economy). While this idea, known as monetarism, was one of Milton Friedman's greatest areas of contribution to the field of economics over the course of his career, it features less prominently in *Capitalism and Freedom*. Friedman would expand upon his ideas on monetarism in his book *A Monetary History of the United States, 1867–1960* (1963), published a year after *Capitalism and Freedom*.[4]

*Capitalism and Freedom* is undoubtedly a general attack on what Friedman believes to be faux (fake or watered-down) liberalism, including the Keynesian* idea of the relationship between government and the people. Interestingly, however, specific Keynesian economic doctrines do not feature prominently in the book. Friedman's arguments concerning money constitute one of the few exceptions, insofar as they directly refute a specific Keynesian policy and present an alternative to it. This policy is that of the government increasing the economy's money supply (by increasing government spending) as a way of generating demand for consumer goods and, consequently, increasing employment and economic growth. Chapters 3 and 5 of *Capitalism and Freedom* present the argument that increasing the money supply causes inflation and unemployment, and that government spending does not expand the economy. Instead, Friedman argues, the best way to grow the economy is to cut government spending. Friedman cites a wide body of research and evidence for this, but for the sake of brevity does not present it in detail.

## NOTES

1   Milton Friedman, *Capitalism and Freedom* (London: University of Chicago Press, 1962), 2.

2   Friedman, *Capitalism and Freedom*, 9.

3   Friedman, *Capitalism and Freedom*, 201.

4   Milton Friedman and Anna J. Schwartz, *A Monetary History of the United States, 1867–1960* (Princeton, NJ: Princeton University Press, 1963).

# ACHIEVEMENT

## KEY POINTS

- While the ideas Milton Friedman develops in *Capitalism and Freedom* have become very influential in economics* and political* philosophy, only a few of his specific proposals were ever adopted in public policy* (that is, only a few were enacted by government).

- Although the text's ideas were not well received at the time of the book's publication, Friedman considered himself to be at the forefront of the discipline of economics.

- While *Capitalism and Freedom*'s core ideas are universal, the book is written to cater primarily to an American audience.

### Assessing the Argument

Milton Friedman's *Capitalism and Freedom* was published in 1962, sufficiently long ago to offer the opportunity of assessing its arguments with hindsight. At the end of his second chapter, Friedman outlines 14 specific policy areas that would be managed better in the private sector* (that is, by private individuals or corporations) rather than through government control. These areas are:

- Intervention to support agricultural prices.
- Tariffs* on trade (that is, taxes imposed on a country's imports or exports).
- Control of economic output (the production of wealth).
- Rent control* (meaning regulation of rental prices in the housing market)
- Legally mandated minimum wage.*

> ❝ A number of economists played important roles in the great revival of classical economics between 1950 and 2000, but none was as influential as Milton Friedman. ❞
>
> Paul Krugman, "Who Was Milton Friedman?" *New York Review of Books*

- Detailed regulation of industries.
- Regulation of radio and television.
- Social security* programs (that is, systems of public insurance to safeguard the welfare of individual citizens).
- Occupational licensure.*
- Public housing* (housing rented at subsidized rates).
- Military service.
- National parks.
- The postal sector.
- Toll roads.

The policy areas in the list, Friedman notes, are "far from comprehensive," but they are used as a framework through which he builds his case in the remaining chapters.[1]

Friedman makes strong arguments for turning all of these policies over to market* control, even if in many instances they are presented as theory rather than fact supported by incontrovertible evidence. Many of his recommendations (for example, the suspension of the minimum wage, deregulation of industries, and the handing over of postal services to private enterprise) have been adopted and have found some success in liberal democracies since the book's publication. However, the majority have either failed to become state policy or, as in the case of trade tariffs, been notionally accepted but frequently violated.

## Achievement in Context

Milton Friedman originally developed the ideas he expounds in *Capitalism and Freedom* in a series of academic lectures in 1956.[2] At the time, the worlds of academia and policymaking were generally hostile to these ideas, and this remained the case at the time of the book's publication in 1962. The work was considered to lie on the fringes of mainstream economic thought, to the extent that it was not reviewed by major news outlets in the years immediately following its release.

Friedman, however, viewed his position at the margin of the debate optimistically. He saw himself at the forefront, rather than the fringe. In the preface to a later edition of *Capitalism and Freedom*, he writes that the function of academics is "to develop alternatives to existing policies, to keep them alive and available until the politically impossible becomes politically inevitable."[3]

Following the book's publication, Friedman's interpretation of his own contribution to the discipline was proven correct over several decades. The significance of *Capitalism and Freedom* did not change as a result of new discoveries in economics—over the last half-century, economists have published innumerable studies and writings both in support of and in opposition to Friedman. Rather, *Capitalism and Freedom*'s steady increase in significance was the result of a change in the political climate surrounding academia. In this respect, the decades following the book's publication saw the end of communism* and the rise of market fundamentalism*—a particularly uncompromising belief in the superiority of the free market—in the Western world.

## Limitations

One of *Capitalism and Freedom*'s greatest limitations is that the book is written chiefly for an American audience. While the political philosophies Friedman invokes are universal (and primarily European in their origin), the vast majority of the book is devoted to applying them to an American domestic context. Furthermore, Keynesianism,* against which Friedman positions many of his arguments, was also formulated in Europe. On the one hand, Friedman's book is important insofar as it introduces a debate involving European ideas to the average American. On the other hand, this prevents the book from being accessible to readers abroad. Friedman's later publications gained global fame, but his desire to appeal to Americans first is one explanation as to why his ideas have become so prominent in North America but continue to be seen as radical, or even dangerous, by audiences in Europe today.

Another limitation of the book is the discrepancy evident in it between Friedman's stated views on the inseparable nature of economic freedom and political freedom and the way that he prioritizes one idea over the other. On the one hand, Friedman writes in his 2002 preface to the 40th-anniversary edition of *Capitalism and Freedom* that political and economic freedom are not wholly separate things.[4] On the other hand, the book clearly goes on to show the reader that, to the liberal idealist, economics ought to be the first and most essential concern. Friedman spends the bulk of the book elaborating on the role of economic forces in creating a better, freer society. Friedman does *not* aim to show that economically free societies must be politically free; rather, he aims to show that politically free societies cannot be so without economic freedom.

## NOTES

1   Milton Friedman, *Capitalism and Freedom* (London: University of Chicago Press, 1962), 36.

2   Friedman, *Capitalism and Freedom*, vii.

3   Friedman, *Capitalism and Freedom*, xiv.

4   Friedman, *Capitalism and Freedom*, xvii.

# MODULE 8
# PLACE IN THE AUTHOR'S WORK

## KEY POINTS

- Milton Friedman's life's work was built on the idea that human beings should be economically and politically free beings.

- *Capitalism and Freedom* incorporates much of Friedman's past research in economics* and repackages it as a polemic.*

- Friedman spent much of the rest of his career elaborating on the ideas presented in *Capitalism and Freedom*.

### Positioning

While *Capitalism and Freedom* is Milton Friedman's most notable work, it is far from his first. Friedman was already a well-known economist by the time the book was published. *Capitalism and Freedom* followed on from a large body of work that Friedman developed, often with fellow Chicago School* economists. This body of work covered the following subjects:

- Macroeconomics* (the study of the economy as a whole).
- Price theory* (the idea that price levels are a reflection of the interaction between forces of demand and supply).
- Monetary theory* (the process by which a government, usually through a central bank, controls the amount of money in circulation).

Friedman's first major work was *Income from Independent Professional Practice* (1945),[1] which he coauthored with the American economist Simon Kuznets.* The book is concerned with regulation of

> **❝ *Capitalism and Freedom* … is Friedman's greatest work in political philosophy. ❞**
> Herbert Gintis, "Review of Milton Friedman, *Capitalism and Freedom*"

professional practice, a microeconomic* issue (that is, an issue concerning economics on the level of the individual or the community). While Friedman's early interest in economics was in the area of microeconomic theory, by the 1950s he began to devote his attention to macroeconomics. His 1957 book *A Theory of the Consumption Function*[2] was his first major foray into macroeconomics, and it proved to be a landmark book in challenging Keynesianism,* the academic consensus of the time.

A year after *Capitalism and Freedom*'s publication, Friedman coauthored *A Monetary History of the United States, 1867–1960* (1963) with the economist Anna J. Schwartz.*[3] While *Capitalism and Freedom* would eventually become hugely influential in anti-Keynesian political and economic ideology,* *A Monetary History* is seen as one of Friedman's most impactful books within the discipline of economics. His receipt of the Nobel Prize in Economic Sciences* in 1976, however, is directly attributed to his other works in consumption theory* (the study of the relationship between income and consumption) and monetary history.

## Integration

*Capitalism and Freedom* was written two decades after Friedman had begun practicing as a professional economist. His arguments by this point drew on considerable experience. Consequently, the book integrates his previous work comprehensively. *Capitalism and Freedom*'s chapter on occupational licensure* draws directly on Friedman's 1945 book with Kuznets, *Income from Independent Professional Practice*. In that book, the authors make a case for the end of government-regulated licensing for professions, such as the medical profession. They argue that licensing unnecessarily creates barriers for entry to the profession and raises prices for consumers. It is better, the authors claim, to let the market* regulate professions and leave pricing to open competition. *Income from Independent Professional Practice* runs to nearly 600 pages, but in *Capitalism and Freedom* the argument, which is one of the more radical ideas in the book, is condensed to a single chapter. Friedman also uses the argument to reinforce his broader thesis about the inferiority of government control compared with market forces.

*Capitalism and Freedom* also represents Friedman taking his anti-Keynesian stance to the next level—he had previously developed this stance most significantly in *A Theory of the Consumption Function* (1957). In *Capitalism and Freedom*, Friedman brings his macroeconomic views into the political arena and challenges Keynesianism on both political and economic grounds.

### Significance

*Capitalism and Freedom* has sold over half a million copies around the world, and has been translated into 18 languages.[4] The book represents a turning point in Friedman's evolution from a professional economist into a public intellectual. *Capitalism and Freedom* has chapters spanning a diverse range of issues, and it can be seen as a unification of various strands of Friedman's research in economics into a single thesis. As such, *Capitalism and Freedom* is the first step in collating the opinions Friedman formulated in the process of his research into multiple fields of economics into a coherent ideological viewpoint. His arguments went on to fuel the rise of several political ideologies, including modern-day conservatism* and libertarianism,* in many countries around the world.

*Capitalism and Freedom* is also significant in the body of Friedman's work as a foundation upon which he could elaborate his teachings. The book gave rise to a large body of writing from Friedman. This includes his later book, *Free to Choose* (1980), which served as the basis for a television series. While *Capitalism and Freedom* was received with little attention in 1962, it would eventually become a core work around which academics, and those with a general interest in the Chicago School, could develop their understanding further.

## NOTES

1   Milton Friedman and Simon Kuznets, *Income from Independent Professional Practice* (New York: National Bureau for Economic Research, 1945).

2   Milton Friedman, *A Theory of the Consumption Function* (Princeton, NJ: Princeton University Press, 1957).

3   Milton Friedman and Anna J. Schwartz, *A Monetary History of the United States, 1867–1960* (Princeton, NJ: Princeton University Press, 1963).

4   Brian Doherty, *Radicals for Capitalism: A Freewheeling History of the Modern American Libertarian Movement* (New York: Public Affairs, 2008), 301.

# SECTION 3
## IMPACT

# THE FIRST RESPONSES

## KEY POINTS

- *Capitalism and Freedom* was largely ignored by critics when it was first published in 1962, though Milton Friedman's ideas in the book would later draw more criticism as he became increasingly famous.

- Friedman responded to his critics by debating them in the public arena as his career progressed.

- Although Friedman and his critics did not reach a consensus, public opinion and policymaking shifted in Friedman's favor within two decades of *Capitalism and Freedom*'s publication.

### Criticism

When Milton Friedman first published *Capitalism and Freedom* in 1962, the text was initially met with mixed reviews. Among academic publications the text was given negative reviews,[1] and outside of academia, the book was largely ignored.[2] For example, almost no major news publications reviewed it, with the British economic journal the *Economist** standing out as a notable exception. A 1963 review in the *Economist* stated that the book had "very considerable merits" and "makes ideal reading for politicians … because it challenges the reader to sort out his own ideas more fundamentally."[3] Even this review did not assess the validity of Friedman's ideas as a contribution to economic policy. Instead, it praised their courage in standing up to prevailing doctrines.

The *Economist*'s review was critical of Friedman's extremism, believing that as a consequence the book's ideas were difficult for most

> **❝** I must say that I find it slightly revolting that people sneer at a system that's made it possible for them to sneer at it. **❞**
>
> Milton Friedman, in Michael Laurence and Geoffrey Norman, "Milton Friedman: The Playboy Interview," *Playboy*

readers to relate to and provoked arguments that were too simplistic. One of *Capitalism and Freedom*'s early academic reviewers, the University of Chicago professor Frank Breul,* echoed these sentiments. However, Breul insisted that Friedman's extremism came from a "man of good will who has a strong social conscience and who believes sincerely that attempts at reform over the last 50 years [1912–62] have done more harm than good."[4]

## Responses

As *Capitalism and Freedom* lacked many direct critics, Friedman's concern was to respond to the continued dominance of Keynesianism* in the two decades after his book's publication. This response came most significantly in the form of *Free to Choose* (1980), a book and 10-part television series that was "a direct lineal descendant of *Capitalism and Freedom* presenting the same basic philosophy."[5]

The television series was framed as a direct rebuttal of a 1977 television series by the Canadian American economist John Kenneth Galbraith,* *The Age of Uncertainty*, which justified the Keynesian perspective to a mainstream audience growing accustomed to receiving its news from the television. Friedman noted in 1982 that the biggest validation of his point of view against Keynesianism was "experience, not theory or philosophy."[6] He cited the decline of Russia and China, the "deep trouble" faced by socialist* public policy* in Britain, and American disillusionment from the great loss of life and military defeat in the Vietnam War* (1955–75) as evidence of the inability of big government to steer society to prosperity.[7] Most significantly, Friedman wrote that "reform programs" such as welfare, public housing,* support of trade unions* (organizations founded by workers to safeguard their interests through collective action and negotiation), the racial integration of schools, federal aid to education, and affirmative action* (that is, the formal policy to favor members of discriminated groups) were all "turning to ashes" by the 1980s.[8]

## Conflict and Consensus

Milton Friedman and his critics never reconciled their viewpoints or reached a consensus. This is a testament to the uncompromising nature of the debate. For Friedman, true liberalism* requires nothing short of a full commitment to individualism matched with a deep-seated skepticism of government. True liberalism requires unwillingness on the part of the liberal to make the concessions already made by Keynesianism, a consensus-building ideology* made by balancing social and individual needs.

Some arguments made in *Capitalism and Freedom* were eventually given weight by the economic events that would come to pass in the decades after the book's publication. "The climate of opinion," Friedman would later reflect, "received a further boost … when the Berlin Wall* fell in 1989 and the Soviet Union* collapsed in 1992."[9] (The Berlin Wall, built in 1961, was a militarized border between East and West Berlin, divided following the end of World War II* in 1945; the West was democratic and capitalist, the East nominally communist, and authoritarian, in that citizens faced intrusive government without recourse to elections.) But Friedman's critics never conceded to his perspective, and his views continued to face opposition throughout the twentieth century. However, within two decades of *Capitalism and Freedom*'s publication, the tides of public opinion and policymaking had clearly shifted in the direction of Friedman's arguments. He had become a household name, and this attracted the attention of politicians and policymakers.

Friedman's overwhelming support from within the American and British governments of President Ronald Reagan* and Prime Minister Margaret Thatcher* respectively led to the realization of his ideas in public policy and the global economic system. This drew new generations of economists and policymakers toward Friedman's camp, stifling the debate in Friedman's favor until the 2000s.

## NOTES

1   William Ruger, *Milton Friedman* (London: Bloomsbury Academic, 2013), 173.

2   Ruger, *Milton Friedman*, 173.

3   *Economist*, "A Tract for the Times," February 16, 1963, accessed January 6, 2016, http://www.economist.com/node/8311321.

4   Frank R. Breul, "Capitalism and Freedom: An Essay Review," *Social Service Review* 37, no. 2 (June 1963): 201.

5   Milton Friedman, *Capitalism and Freedom* (40th Anniversary Edition) (London: University of Chicago Press, 2002), xii.

6   Friedman, *Capitalism and Freedom*, xii.

7   Friedman, *Capitalism and Freedom*, xii.

8   Friedman, *Capitalism and Freedom*, xii.

9   Friedman, *Capitalism and Freedom*, xii.

# MODULE 10
# THE EVOLVING DEBATE

## KEY POINTS

- Published in 1962, *Capitalism and Freedom* presented ideas that went on to become very popular and influential in shaping the policy debates of the 1970s and 1980s.

- Milton Friedman's ideas in the book were integral to the formulation of economic schools of thought, such as monetarism,* and important political movements of the twentieth century.

- Friedman is one of the most cited economists of recent times, and today *Capitalism and Freedom* is regarded as the foundation text for his subsequent body of work.

### Uses and Problems

Many of Milton Friedman's ideas in *Capitalism and Freedom* have gained enduring appeal in the last several decades. This is a result both of their usefulness and of the economic and policy problems that arose from government interventionism. While many scholars took up Friedman's views, Friedman himself was their main champion. His towering stature in the field meant that he continued to be the principal proponent of his own economic ideas until his death in 2006.

A good example is *Capitalism and Freedom*'s argument concerning fiscal* and monetary policy* (fiscal policy relates to taxation and government spending, while monetary policy is the process by which a government controls the amount of money in circulation). Friedman's argument received much attention during the period of stagflation* (that is, the simultaneous occurrence of inflation,* high

> ❝ The profession [of economics]* has gone very much to the right ideologically.* And guess who was the most important person responsible for that ... it was Milton Friedman. ❞
>
> Paul Samuelson, in Karen Ilse Horn, *Roads to Wisdom, Conversations with Ten Nobel Laureates*

levels of unemployment, and sluggish economic growth) experienced in the United States during the second half of the 1970s. Stagflation seriously undermined Keynesianism,* which taught that inflation-causing government spending was an important tool in lowering unemployment levels. Friedman's ideas provided alternatives. In a later preface to *Capitalism and Freedom*, written in 1982, Friedman says, "Only a crisis—actual or perceived—produces real change ... That, I believe, is [economists' and policymakers'] basic function: to develop alternatives to existing policies."[1] *Capitalism and Freedom*'s arguments on fiscal and monetary policy were developed further by Friedman in later books and in his 1980 television series *Free to Choose*, which was immensely popular.

*Capitalism and Freedom*'s arguments in favor of free trade* also developed considerable influence. The link between democracy and free markets* was a driving force in developing the rationale behind global free-trade regimes. Friedman's ideas played a large role in the United States' decision to end the Bretton Woods System,* the international monetary regime that had pegged the value of global currencies to a fixed quantity of gold. This system was a significant barrier to free trade, which requires flexible convertibility between currencies.

## Schools of Thought

*Capitalism and Freedom* went on to influence several political and economic schools of thought. One of these, monetarism, remains central to the Chicago School* tradition. Some of its core ideas have become accepted by the mainstream today.[2] Among other things, monetarism teaches that increasing government spending causes inflation without really lowering unemployment. Friedman introduces these ideas in the book's fifth chapter.

Friedman discusses the issue of military conscription* in several parts of *Capitalism and Freedom*. Conscription is the mandatory enlisting of certain citizens into the armed forces. One of his 14 policy recommendations in the book specifically calls for an end to conscription and its replacement with a market* for people to serve in the armed forces voluntarily. Friedman would later serve on the Gates Commission,* the body tasked to produce a report on the feasibility of ending conscription, which eventually persuaded the United States government to end the draft in 1973.[3]

*Capitalism and Freedom* was also highly influential in the development of both political conservatism* and libertarianism* in Great Britain and the United States during the last decades of the twentieth century. The book is frequently cited as an influence on the administrations of Prime Minister Margaret Thatcher* in the United Kingdom and President Ronald Reagan* in the United States, both leading figures in conservative politics* during this period.[4] In his 2008 history of modern libertarian thought, the US journalist Brian Doherty* notes that *Capitalism and Freedom* was "both a great teacher and a great symbol of respectability … to the generation of young libertarians coming of age in the 1960s."[5]

## In Current Scholarship

Since Friedman's death in 2006, no other economist has argued so vigorously and successfully in favor of the free market as the main mediator of human affairs. The economist Robert Solow* has attributed this to the fact that "most economists realize that serious questions in economics are rarely, if ever, single or transparent."[6]

According to Google Scholar, Friedman has been cited in academic publications nearly 35,000 times, and *Capitalism and Freedom* itself has been cited nearly 15,000 times.[7] While Friedman's ideas are no longer championed in the same way, they continue to pervade the discussions of mainstream economics, as well as a diverse range of other social sciences.

Ben Bernanke,* the former chairman of the United States Federal Reserve* (the central bank of the United States), has emphasized Friedman's influence on current scholarship. "Among economic scholars, Milton Friedman had no peer," he said, shortly after Friedman's death in 2006. "The direct and indirect influences of his thinking on contemporary monetary economics would be difficult to overstate."[8] In a study at the end of the 1990s on the most frequently cited living economists of the time, Milton Friedman ranked first, having been cited in every textbook.[9]

## NOTES

1   Milton Friedman, *Capitalism and Freedom* (40th Anniversary Edition) (London: University of Chicago Press, 2002), XIV.

2   Sarwat Jahan and Chris Papageorgiou, "What is Monetarism?" *Finance & Development* 51, no. 1 (2014).

3   Thomas S. Gates, *The Report of the President's Commission on an All-Volunteer Armed Force* (New York: Collier Books, 1970).

4   Richard Posner, "Why Is There No Milton Friedman Today?" *Econ Journal Watch* 10, no. 2 (2013): 210.

5   Brian Doherty, *Radicals for Capitalism: A Freewheeling History of the Modern American Libertarian Movement* (New York: Public Affairs, 2008), 301–2.

6   Robert M. Solow, "Why Is There No Milton Friedman Today?" *Econ Journal Watch* 10, no. 2 (2013): 215.

7    Google Scholar, "Milton Friedman," accessed February 13, 2016, https://scholar.google.com/citations?user=DV6pTH0AAAAJ&hl=en&oi=ao.

8    Board of the Federal Reserve System, "Statement by Federal Reserve Chairman Ben S. Bernanke," November 16, 2006, accessed January 6, 2016, http://www.federalreserve.gov/newsevents/press/other/20061116a.htm.

9    Mark Skousen, "Who is the Greatest Economist of the Twentieth Century?", last modified February 5, 1999, http://mskousen.com/1999/02/who-is-the-greatest-economist-of-the-20th-century.

## MODULE 11
# IMPACT AND INFLUENCE TODAY

## KEY POINTS

- Milton Friedman's *Capitalism and Freedom* is still an important text in conservative political thought.

- The book was a direct challenge to policymakers to reconsider their belief in Keynesianism* and reduce their interference in the free market.*

- The debate between Friedman's supporters and Keynesians continues today, re-energized by the impact of the 2008 Global Financial Crisis*—the greatest economic crisis since the Great Depression* of the 1920s and 1930s.

### Position

Milton Friedman's *Capitalism and Freedom* is considered an important reference text in contemporary political conservatism* and libertarianism.* Friedman was an advisor to Prime Minister Margaret Thatcher* in the United Kingdom and President Ronald Reagan* in the United States.[1] Both of these political administrations were crucial in advancing the conservative political agenda in their respective countries, and their legacies persist to this day. *Capitalism and Freedom* has also been cited as a groundbreaking work in the development of the post-World War II* libertarian movement,[2] which prioritizes individual freedom over any political authority. This movement also remains active.

Friedman's influence extends beyond Europe and North America. For example, in Chile in the 1970s dictator Augusto Pinochet* put free-market policies in place that were designed to transform Chile into a capitalist* country. "The basic free market premises of this

> **❝ I'm enormously gratified by how well the book has withstood the test of time. ❞**
>
> Milton Friedman, 2002 Preface to *Capitalism and Freedom*

economic doctrine," sociologist* George Ritzer* has written, "were derived from Friedman's teachings and writings (especially *Capitalism and Freedom*)."[3] Friedman-inspired economic policies have been credited with turning Chile into South America's most competitive economy, and many of these policies are still in place today.[4]

## Interaction

As a work of political philosophy, *Capitalism and Freedom* presents ideas partial to a particular political agenda. It challenges a range of political ideologies* that threaten individual freedom and free-market economics. Most directly the book challenges Keynesian economists and policymakers on their advocacy of government intervention in the economy and their reluctance to embrace privatization of public affairs. By invoking case studies of real public policies* like military conscription* or healthcare in its chapters, Friedman uses *Capitalism and Freedom* to issue a direct challenge to the policymaking establishment in the United States.

The response of American policymakers to Friedman's ideas has shifted back and forth over time along with the country's political preferences. In the 1970s and early 1980s, a debate over who could influence American public policy was raging between Friedman and proponents of Keynesianism. In 1977, the economist John Kenneth Galbraith* released his book and television series *The Age of Uncertainty*, which made the case for government intervention in the market. In 1980, Friedman countered with his own book and series, *Free to Choose*, which revived many of the arguments he had made in *Capitalism and Freedom*.

By the time of the Ronald Reagan administration in the United States, which began in 1981, policymakers were more receptive to Friedman's position. Reagan even appointed Friedman as one of his advisors, and Friedman's ideas continued to dominate American economic policy throughout the 1980s and 1990s, and into the early 2000s. "Eventually," writes the American economist Paul Krugman,* "the anti-Keynesian counterrevolution went far beyond Friedman's position, which came to seem relatively moderate compared with what his successors were saying."[5] Financial economists and macroeconomists* alike all praised the market for its efficiency and advocated for market forces to be the primary driver of public affairs.

## The Continuing Debate

Following the long period of grave tension between the United States and the now-dissolved Soviet Union* known as the Cold War,* Keynesian ideas re-entered the policy mainstream.[6] The 2008 Global Financial Crisis brought about the most significant resurgence of Keynesianism in recent times, with its supporters such as the Nobel Prize*–winning economists Paul Krugman and Joseph Stiglitz* rising in popularity. Friedman's influence on policy in preceding decades has often been cited as a reason behind the crisis.[7] In the same way that Friedman had introduced his ideas as an alternative way of thinking to an American public increasingly disenchanted with Keynesianism, economists had begun to reintroduce Keynesianism as an alternative to Friedman.[8] "We are all Keynesians now," the economics journalist Martin Wolf* wrote in the months after the crisis began.[9]

However, frustration with the weakness of economic recovery, along with new problems, has caused a backlash. The ongoing European Debt Crisis* and the growing frustration with government policy within the American electorate have allowed space for Friedman's ideas once again. "We were all Keynesians," wrote Joseph Stiglitz, "but all too briefly."[10] In Great Britain and Europe, fiscal

austerity*—introducing government cuts rather than spending—
has replaced fiscal stimulus* (government spending).

## NOTES

1  Charles Moore, *Margaret Thatcher: The Authorized Biography, Volume One: Not for Turning* (London: Penguin, 2013), 576–7; and Lanny Ebenstein, *Milton Friedman: A Biography* (London: St. Martin's Griffin, 2009), 208.

2  Tom G. Palmer, *Realizing Freedom: Libertarian Theory, History, and Practice* (Washington, DC: CATO Institute, 2009), 429–30.

3  George Ritzer and Paul Dean, *Globalization: A Basic Text* (Oxford: John Wiley & Sons, 2015), 85.

4  Tania Opazo, "The Boys Who Got to Remake an Economy," *Slate*, January 12, 2016, accessed January 13, 2016, http://www.slate.com/articles/business/moneybox/2016/01/in_chicago_boys_the_story_of_chilean_economists_who_studied_in_america_and.html.

5  Paul Krugman, "How Did Economists Get It So Wrong?" *New York Times*, September 2, 2009, accessed January 5, 2016, http://www.nytimes.com/2009/09/06/magazine/06Economic-t.html.

6  Elgie McFayden, "The Clinton Plan of the 1990s and Economic Growth: An Exercise in Contemporary Keynesian Economics," *Social Science Research Network*, March 10, 2008, accessed January 5, 2016, http://papers.ssrn.com/sol3/papers.cfm?abstract_id=1104926.

7  Andrew Stern, "Financial Crisis Haunts Milton Friedman's Legacy," *Reuters*, October 14, 2008, accessed January 6, 2016, http://www.reuters.com/article/us-financial-friedman-chicago-idUSTRE49D9EJ20081014.

8  Peter S. Goodman, "A Fresh Look at the Apostle of Free Markets," *New York Times*, April 13, 2008, accessed January 5, 2016, http://www.nytimes.com/2008/04/13/weekinreview/13goodman.html.

9  Martin Wolf, "Keynes Offers Us the Best Way to Think About the Financial Crisis," *Financial Times*, December 23, 2008, accessed January 7, 2016, http://www.ft.com/cms/s/0/be2dbf2c-d113-11dd-8cc3-000077b07658.html#axzz3yYYVMwNW.

10 Joseph E. Stiglitz, "After the Financial Crisis, We Were All Keynesians – But Not For Long Enough," *Guardian*, October 10, 2013, accessed January 6, 2016, http://www.theguardian.com/business/economics-blog/2013/oct/10/financial-crisis-keynesians-eurozone-recession.

# WHERE NEXT?

## KEY POINTS

- Recent global economic crises have weakened the position of free-market* economics and shifted the academic consensus toward Keynesianism.*

- Although economists of the Chicago School* have been divided by these events, many of Milton Friedman's ideas still enjoy support.

- As Friedman's first broad work written for the public, *Capitalism and Freedom* plays an important role in representing Friedman's teachings in the ongoing debate between Keynesians and conservative* economists.

### Potential

In 2004, Milton Friedman, author of *Capitalism and Freedom*, told the *Wall Street Journal*\* that the "battle of ideas had been won."[1] But after a resurgence of Keynesianism in the wake of the 2008 Global Financial Crisis,* free-market economics has found itself under threat once again. Recent world events have created considerable hostility toward two particular ideas that exist within the scope of Friedman's view of economics.

The first of these is deregulation of the financial markets. The 2008 Global Financial Crisis and the subsequent European Debt Crisis* have both been attributed to unfettered lending and borrowing among governments and private citizens alike. The American government responded with a mixture of Keynesian policies, such as the government spending described as "fiscal stimulus"* and intervening to prevent the bankruptcy of major financial institutions.

> **❝** [The 2008 Global Financial Crisis]* is a challenge to
> the economics* profession as a whole, but to Chicago
> most of all. **❞**
> Richard Posner,* in John Cassidy,* "After the Blowup," *The New Yorker*

However, fiscal austerity* (that is, prioritizing the reduction of
government budget deficits and the national debt by cutting public
expenditure and paying back loans) has been the favored response
among European governments. This has resulted in a popular backlash
against market fundamentalism*—a dogmatic adherence to free-
market principles. Within academia, there is now a broad agreement in
favor of a Keynesian response to debt crises.

The second idea toward which there is now hostility is that of faith
in the ability of the free market to moderate economic inequality. In
the last few years, several prominent economists have produced works
on the dangers of economic inequality inherent in an unrestrained free
market. These works include the American economist Joseph Stiglitz's*
*The Price of Inequality* (2012), the French economist Thomas Piketty's*
*Capital in the Twenty-First Century* (2013), and the British economist
Anthony Atkinson's* *Inequality: What Can Be Done?* (2014).[2]

### Future Directions

The 2008 Global Financial Crisis began an internal crisis within the
Chicago School of economics. Leading Chicago School economist
Richard Posner switched his allegiance to Keynesianism.[3] Another
Chicago School economist, Nobel Prize*–winner Gary Becker,*
claimed that the crisis demonstrated that "markets don't always work
well."[4]

The British American economics writer John Cassidy has written
that the consensus among conservative economists is not a total loss of
confidence in Friedman's ideas. He recalls two important beliefs of

Chicago economics: that the market will always work efficiently, and that government will always work badly. "The first one has sort of gone out the window, but they do tend to fall back on the second idea that that doesn't mean that governments will do any better."[5]

America's modest but positive recovery from the financial crisis has now made the debate within the Chicago School less urgent.[6] The Keynesian policies of the American government through the crisis also came with higher levels of taxation and other policy decisions associated with the economic left. These policies have combined with the polarization of American politics to re-energize conservative political and economic platforms in the public conversation. Consequently, Milton Friedman's intellectual descendants within the Chicago School may once again see a climate of opinion that is favorable to the ideas he expressed in *Capitalism and Freedom*.

## Summary

Milton Friedman is one of the most influential economists of the twentieth century. *Capitalism and Freedom* marked his transition from an academic economist into a public thinker. The decades after the book was published saw his meteoric rise, culminating in his role advising conservative governments in the United States and the United Kingdom.

Friedman was a leading figure in the development of the Chicago School of economic thought. Under his leadership, the school advanced economic ideas drawn from the political philosophy of classical liberalism.* Friedman considered individual liberty to be paramount, and saw the free market as the best mechanism for providing for people's needs. He argued that, although there is a need for government to exist, its role should be limited.

*Capitalism and Freedom* was Friedman's first presentation of these ideas to the general public. The book supports them with a wide-ranging discussion of public policy.* Friedman identifies several areas of public policy where the market could manage affairs better than government. He also makes a case for limited government interference in the economy's money supply,* an idea that eventually grew into a school of thought known as monetarism.* All of these ideas directly confronted Keynesianism, the dominant economic ideology* of the early twentieth century and a significant force to this day.

*Capitalism and Freedom* served as the basis of much of Friedman's later work, including his highly influential book and television series *Free to Choose* (1980). His ideas brought about a significant shift in mainstream conservative economics, inspiring policies that would transform the nature of the global economy. In recent years, Friedman's ideas have been threatened by ongoing global economic crises that have been attributed to the legacy of his influence. Nonetheless, a renewed debate between conservatives and Keynesians has re-energized free-market thinking.

## NOTES

1   Robert M. Solow, "Hayek, Friedman, and the Illusions of Conservative Economics," *New Republic*, November 16, 2012, accessed January 2, 2016, https://newrepublic.com/article/110196/hayek-friedman-and-the-illusions-conservative-economics.

2   Joseph E. Stiglitz, *The Price of Inequality* (New York: W.W. Norton & Company, 2012); Thomas Piketty, *Capital in the Twenty-First Century* (Cambridge, MA: Harvard University Press, 2013); and Anthony B. Atkinson, *Inequality: What Can Be Done?* (Cambridge, MA: Harvard University Press, 2014).

3   John Cassidy, "After the Blowup," *New Yorker*, January 11, 2010, accessed January 2, 2016, http://www.newyorker.com/magazine/2010/01/11/after-the-blowup.

4   Kai Ryssdal, "Chicago School of Economics Post-Crisis: Interview with John Cassidy," *Marketplace*, January 7, 2010, accessed January 2, 2016, http://www.marketplace.org/2010/01/07/business/fallout-financial-crisis/chicago-school-economics-post-crisis.

5   Ryssdal, "Chicago School of Economics Post-Crisis."

6   Ryssdal, "Chicago School of Economics Post-Crisis."

# GLOSSARY

# GLOSSARY OF TERMS

**2008 Global Financial Crisis:** the most serious financial crisis since the Great Depression. The crisis was caused by the collapse of the American housing bubble and resulted in mass defaults on debts, affecting financial institutions and markets worldwide.

**Affirmative action:** a formal policy to favor members of a historically discriminated group.

**Austrian School:** a school of economic thought that focuses on the rationality and actions of individuals as the primary unit of economic analysis.

**Berlin Wall:** this wall—guarded at checkpoints by armed soldiers—separated East and West Berlin from 1961 to 1989. It was built by the East German government to prevent its citizens from defecting to the West.

**Boom and bust:** a characteristic of capitalist economic systems in which the economy switches between phases of dramatic expansion and contraction.

**Bretton Woods System:** the international monetary regime that prevailed from 1944 until 1971 in which global currencies were pegged to gold. The International Monetary Fund was created to intervene when an imbalance of payments occurred.

**Capitalism:** economic and political system in which factors of production (generally tools and resources) are controlled by private owners for profit, rather than by the state.

**Chicago School:** a school of economic thought that originated at the University of Chicago. It argues for the primacy of the free market, as well as for disciplined fiscal policy.

**Classical liberalism:** a political philosophy that originated in the period of European intellectual and cultural history known as the Enlightenment (in the seventeenth and eighteenth centuries). It emphasizes individual liberty, equality, and economic freedom.

**Cold War:** a period of political tension, military hostility, and economic and technological competition between the United States, the Soviet Union, and their respective allies that lasted from 1945 to 1990.

**Columbia University:** a private university in New York City, founded in 1754.

**Communism:** a political ideology advocating common ownership of the means of production and the destruction of social hierarchy.

**Conscription:** a policy of mandatory enlistment of certain citizens into the armed forces.

**Conservatism:** an umbrella term encompassing a collection of political philosophies that value tradition and are skeptical of proposals for change. More recently in Western democracies, conservatism also includes advocacy of free-market economic policies.

**Consumer budget survey:** a national survey of average consumer spending.

**Consumption theory:** a field of study within economics concerned with the relationship between income and consumption.

**Economics:** a discipline of the social sciences that studies human behavior and social systems under conditions of scarce means and unlimited wants.

*Economist*: an English-language weekly newspaper covering political and economic affairs, established in London in 1843.

**Enlightenment:** a period of European intellectual and cultural history, at its height in the late seventeenth century and the eighteenth century, that gave rise to a philosophical movement emphasizing liberty, equality, and reason.

**European Debt Crisis:** an ongoing debt crisis within the European Union in which several member states have been unable to repay loans to private and public creditors.

**Fascism:** a political system headed and controlled by a dictator that permits no opposition.

**Fiscal austerity:** a set of economic policies that prioritize the reduction of government budget deficits and the national debt by cutting public expenditure and paying back loans.

**Fiscal policy:** policies concerned with government spending and taxation.

**Fiscal stimulus:** an economic policy in which the government increases its share of debt in the economy by raising its level of spending or lowering taxes, usually as a means of encouraging the public to spend more and grow the economy.

**Flat tax:** a policy of maintaining a consistent and proportional rate of taxation across individuals or corporations.

**Free-floating exchange rate:** a regime of currency regulation in which the nominal values of currencies are allowed to fluctuate with market conditions.

**Free market:** an economic system typified by a minimally regulated market for goods and services.

**Free trade:** unrestricted exchange of goods or services between the citizens of different countries.

**Gates Commission:** a group of professionals and public intellectuals tasked by the United States President Richard Nixon with exploring the feasibility of transitioning the American military to an all-volunteer force.

**Great Depression:** a period of extreme economic downturn that affected the entire industrialized world from 1929 to 1939.

**Ideology:** a system of beliefs.

**Income distribution:** the allocation of an economy's total output or wealth among its population.

**Inflation:** an increase in the general level of prices in an economy.

**Keynesianism:** an economic school of thought developed by the British economist John Maynard Keynes during the 1930s. It teaches that in the short term a country's economic output is influenced by the economy's level of aggregate demand.

**Laissez-faire:** a government policy of supporting a free market by minimizing state involvement in economic affairs.

**Liberalism:** an umbrella term encompassing a collection of political philosophies united by a common focus on individual liberty and equality between people.

**Libertarianism:** a political philosophy that is principally concerned with protecting individual liberty.

**Macroeconomics:** a branch of study in economics concerned with the economy as a whole.

**Market:** an economic system characterized by parties engaging in exchange.

**Market fundamentalism:** an uncompromising belief in the superiority of the free market as a means of improving social and economic life.

**Microeconomics:** a branch of study in economics concerned with the economic behavior of individuals.

**Minimum wage:** a government-legislated universal baseline level for employee wages.

**Monetarism:** a school of thought within economics that emphasizes the economic effects of government involvement in the money supply.

**Monetary policy:** the process by which a government, usually through a central bank, controls the amount of money circulating in the economy.

**Monetary theory:** a field of study within economics concerned with the role of money, as well as the quantity and regulation of money, in the economy.

**Money supply:** the quantity of money circulating in the economy.

**Monopoly:** an economic state in which a single person or entity exerts total or near-total control over a given commodity.

**Mont Pelerin Society:** an international think tank and discussion group concerned with furthering understanding of political and economic freedom.

**Natural Resources Committee:** a committee within the legislative branch of American government concerned with natural resource management policies.

**New Deal:** an extensive American government program enacted between 1933 and 1938 by President Franklin D. Roosevelt. It utilized fiscal stimulus and large-scale government intervention in the economy to combat the effects of the Great Depression.

**Nobel Prize in Economics:** an international award given for outstanding contributions to the discipline of economics.

**Occupational licensure:** regulation requiring government-recognized licenses to practice given professions.

**Oligarchy:** a system of government in which power, by law or in practice, rests with a small elite.

**Paternalism:** the practice of the people in authority restricting the freedom and responsibilities of subordinate individuals in their supposed interest.

**Polemic:** a piece of writing that directly attacks an opinion or theory, intended to persuade readers of the writer's point of view.

**Political economy:** an area of study that examines the relationship between political and economic forces.

**Politics:** activities related to governance, power relations, and the state, as well as the academic study of these activities.

**Poverty:** a condition in which one lacks a minimum level of resources, determined as either a relative or an absolute measure, to achieve a necessary quality of life.

**Price theory:** the idea within the discipline of economics that price levels are a reflection of the interaction between forces of demand and supply.

**Private enterprise:** for-profit businesses owned by private individuals or corporations.

**Private sector:** the section of an economy consisting of private enterprises and controlled by private individuals or corporations, rather than nonprofit groups, public entities, or government.

**Public housing:** a form of housing owned by the government and rented to tenants at subsidized rates.

**Public policy:** the process of formulating government policy regarding the evolution of laws and customs.

**Quantitative analysis:** the analysis of a situation, especially a financial market, by using complex mathematical and statistical modeling and research in an attempt to understand behavior.

**Rent control:** government regulation of rental prices in the housing market.

**Rutgers University:** a public university in New Jersey, USA, founded in 1766.

**Socialism:** a political ideology advocating social or democratic control over an economy's resources.

**Social liberalism:** a suite of beliefs in which the government is understood to serve a vital role in ensuring equality, prosperity, and standards, and access to things such as education and healthcare.

**Social security:** a system of public insurance to safeguard the welfare of individual citizens.

**Sociology:** the study of the nature and functioning of human society, and of social behavior more generally.

**Soviet Union:** officially titled the Union of Soviet Socialist Republics (USSR), the Soviet Union was a superstate between 1922 and 1991. Located in Eastern Europe and northwestern Asia, its capital was Moscow.

**Stagflation:** an economic condition in which a given economy experiences stagnation and inflation simultaneously.

**Sweatshop:** a factory or workshop, particularly in the clothing industry, where workers endure long hours for low pay in poor conditions.

**Tariff:** a tax imposed on a country's imports or exports.

**Trade union:** an organization of traders, workers, or laborers who join together to protect the integrity of their trade and the standards of their employment.

**United States Federal Reserve:** the central bank of the United States of America.

**University of Chicago:** a public university in Illinois, USA, founded in 1890.

**Vietnam War:** an armed conflict between the United States and pro-communist forces in Vietnam, lasting from 1955 to 1975.

*Wall Street Journal:* a business-focused English-language newspaper based in New York City. It was founded in 1889.

**World War II:** a global armed conflict that lasted from 1939 to 1945, fought between the Allies (led by the Soviet Union, the United Kingdom, and the United States) and the Axis forces (led by Germany, Japan, and Italy).

# PEOPLE MENTIONED IN THE TEXT

**Anthony Atkinson (b. 1944)** is a British economist and a professor at the London School of Economics. He is a leading thinker in the areas of inequality and poverty.

**Gary Becker (1930–2014)** was an American economist at the University of Chicago. He was a prominent figure in the Chicago School of economics.

**Ben Bernanke (b. 1953)** is an American economist. He is the former chairman of the United States Federal Reserve.

**Frank Breul (1916–86)** was an American sociologist and a professor at the University of Chicago.

**Arthur Burns (1904–87)** was an American economist. He taught Milton Friedman at Rutgers University.

**John Cassidy (b. 1963)** is a British American journalist. He writes about economic history and the financial sector.

**Brian Doherty (b. 1968)** is an American journalist. He has written extensively on libertarianism and the history of the libertarian movement.

**John Kenneth Galbraith (1908–2006)** was a Canadian American economist and diplomat. He was a rival of Milton Friedman, and a staunch supporter of Keynesianism.

**Thomas Hill Green (1836–82)** was a nineteenth-century British political philosopher and founder of British idealism.

**Friedrich von Hayek (1899–1992)** was an Austrian British economist. He was a leading figure in the Austrian School of economics.

**Thomas Hobbes (1588–1679)** was a seventeenth-century English political philosopher. He was one of the earliest developers of European liberal thought.

**John Hobson (1858–1940)** was a British economist and liberal thinker.

**John Maynard Keynes (1883–1946)** was a British economist and the founder of Keynesianism. He is considered to be one of the most influential economists in history.

**Frank Knight (1885–1972)** was an American economist. He was one of the founders of the Chicago School of economics.

**Paul Krugman (b. 1953)** is a Nobel Prize–winning American economist. He is a prominent supporter of Keynesian economics.

**Simon Kuznets (1901–85)** was an American economist and Nobel Prize winner. He is known for his work on economic growth and for employing quantitative methods in the study of economic history.

**John Locke (1632–1704)** was an English philosopher during the Enlightenment era. He is considered to be the father of liberalism.

**Thomas Paine (1737–1809)** was a British American political activist and revolutionary. He is one of the Founding Fathers of the United States.

**Thomas Piketty (b. 1971)** is a French economist. He is best known for his work highlighting the propensity of unrestricted capitalism to result in economic and social inequality.

**Augusto Pinochet (1915–2006)** was military dictator of Chile between 1973 and 1990. Although notorious for the mass atrocities committed under his command, he is credited with transforming Chile into a capitalist country.

**Richard Posner (b. 1939)** is an American economist and jurist. Formerly a leading figure in the Chicago School of economics, he now supports the Keynesian view.

**Ronald Reagan (1911–2004)** was president of the United States from 1981 to 1989. His administration came to define modern American political conservatism.

**George Ritzer (b. 1940)** is an American sociologist. He is known for his work on globalization and theory of consumption.

**Franklin D. Roosevelt (1882–1945)** was president of the United States from 1933 to 1945. He implemented Keynesian economic policies, including the New Deal, one of the most extensive programs of government intervention in the American economy's history.

**Joseph Schumpeter (1883–1950)** was an Austrian American economist. He was a staunch supporter of capitalism and the free market.

**Anna J. Schwartz (1915–2012)** was an American economist. She is known for having coauthored a seminal book on monetary theory and history with Milton Friedman.

**Henry Simons (1899–1946)** was an American economist at the University of Chicago. He was one of the founders of the Chicago School of economics.

**Adam Smith (1723–90)** was a Scottish philosopher and political economist. He is considered the father of the discipline of economics, having authored its first major work.

**Robert Solow (b. 1924)** is an American economist. He is known for his groundbreaking work in formulating theories of economic growth.

**Joseph Stiglitz (b. 1943)** is an American economist and a Nobel Prize winner, and was chief economist of the World Bank from 1997 to 2000. He is known for his criticism of neoliberal development policies following his departure from the World Bank.

**Margaret Thatcher (1925–2013)** was prime minister of the United Kingdom from 1979 to 1990. Her economic reforms of the 1980s were inspired by the work of Milton Friedman.

**Jacob Viner (1892–1970)** was a Canadian economist at the University of Chicago. He was one of the founders of the Chicago School of economics.

**Martin Wolf (b. 1946)** is a British journalist, chief economics commentator at the *Financial Times*, and considered to be one of the world's most prominent writers on economics.

# WORKS CITED

# WORKS CITED

Atkinson, Anthony B. *Inequality: What Can Be Done?* Cambridge, MA: Harvard University Press, 2014.

Breul, Frank R. "Capitalism and Freedom: An Essay Review." *Social Service Review* 37, no. 2 (June 1963): 201.

Burton, John, *Twelve Contemporary Economists*. London: Palgrave Macmillan, 1981.

Butler, Eamonn F. *Milton Friedman: A Concise Guide to the Ideas and Influence of the Free Market Economist*. Petersfield: Harriman House Ltd, 2011.

Cassidy, John. "After the Blowup." *New Yorker*, January 11, 2010. Accessed January 2, 2016. http://www.newyorker.com/magazine/2010/01/11/after-the-blowup.

Doherty, Brian. *Radicals for Capitalism: A Freewheeling History of the Modern American Libertarian Movement*. New York: Public Affairs, 2008.

Ebenstein, Lanny. *Milton Friedman: A Biography*. London: St. Martin's Griffin, 2009.

*Economist*. "A Tract for the Times." February 16, 1963. Accessed January 6, 2016. http://www.economist.com/node/8311321.

"Keynes and Hayek: Prophets for Today," March 14, 2014. Accessed January 5, 2016. http://www.economist.com/blogs/freeexchange/2014/03/keynes-and-hayek.

Friedman, Milton. *A Theory of the Consumption Function*. Princeton, NJ: Princeton University Press, 1957.

*Capitalism and Freedom*. London: University of Chicago Press, 1962.

*Tyranny of the Status Quo*. London: Houghton Mifflin Harcourt, 1984.

Interview by Brian Lamb. *Milton Friedman: 50th Anniversary Edition of F. A. Hayek's Road to Serfdom*. C-SPAN Booknotes, November 20, 1994. http://www.c-span.org/video/?61272-1/book-discussion-road-serfdom

*Capitalism and Freedom* (40th Anniversary Edition). London: University of Chicago Press, 2002.

Friedman, Milton, and Rose Friedman. *Free to Choose: A Personal Statement* (New York: Harcourt, Inc, 1980).

Friedman, Milton, and Simon Kuznets. *Income from Independent Professional Practice*. New York: National Bureau for Economic Research, 1945.

Friedman, Milton, and Anna J. Schwartz. *A Monetary History of the United States, 1867–1960*. Princeton, NJ: Princeton University Press, 1963.

Gates, Thomas S. *The Report of the President's Commission on an All-Volunteer Armed Force*. New York: Collier Books, 1970.

Gintis, Herbert. "Review of Milton Friedman, Capitalism and Freedom." Accessed January 4, 2016. http://people.umass.edu/~gintis/papers_index.html.

Goodman, Peter S. "A Fresh Look at the Apostle of Free Markets." *New York Times*, April 13, 2008. Accessed January 5, 2016. http://www.nytimes.com/2008/04/13/weekinreview/13goodman.html.

Hayek, Friedrich. *The Road to Serfdom*. London: Routledge, 1944.

Horn, Karen Ilse. *Roads to Wisdom: Conversations with Ten Nobel Laureates in Economics*. Cheltenham: Edward Elgar Publishing Ltd, 2009.

Ip, Greg, and Mark Whitehouse. "How Milton Friedman Challenged Economics, Policy and Markets," *Wall Street Journal*, November 17, 2006. Accessed January 5, 2016. http://www.wsj.com/articles/SB116369744597625238.

Jahan, Sarwat, and Chris Papageorgiou. "What is Monetarism?" *Finance & Development* 51, no. 1 (2014).

Keynes, John Maynard. *The General Theory of Employment, Interest, and Money*. London: Palgrave Macmillan, 1936.

Krugman, Paul. "Who Was Milton Friedman?" *New York Review of Books*, February 15, 2007.

"How Did Economists Get It So Wrong?" *New York Times*, September 2, 2009. Accessed January 5, 2016. http://www.nytimes.com/2009/09/06/magazine/06Economic-t.html.

Laurence, Michael, and Norman Geoffrey. "Milton Friedman: The Playboy Interview." *Playboy*, February 1973.

McFayden, Elgie. "The Clinton Plan of the 1990s and Economic Growth: An Exercise in Contemporary Keynesian Economics." *Social Science Research Network*, March 10, 2008. Accessed January 5, 2016. http://papers.ssrn.com/sol3/papers.cfm?abstract_id=1104926.

Moore, Charles. *Margaret Thatcher: The Authorized Biography, Volume One: Not for Turning*. London: Penguin, 2013.

Opazo, Tania. "The Boys Who Got to Remake an Economy." *Slate*, January 12, 2016. Accessed January 13, 2016. http://www.slate.com/articles/business/moneybox/2016/01/in_chicago_boys_the_story_of_chilean_economists_who_studied_in_america_and.html.

Paine, Thomas, *Common Sense*. Philadelphia: R. Bell, 1776.

Palmer, Tom G. *Realizing Freedom: Libertarian Theory, History, and Practice*. Washington, DC: CATO Institute, 2009.

Piketty, Thomas, *Capital in the Twenty-First Century*. Cambridge, MA: Harvard University Press, 2013.

Posner, Richard, "Why Is There No Milton Friedman Today?" *Econ Journal Watch* 10, no. 2 (2013).

Ritzer, George, and Paul Dean. *Globalization: A Basic Text*. Oxford: John Wiley & Sons, 2015.

Ruger, William, *Milton Friedman*. London: Bloomsbury Academic, 2013.

Ryssdal, Kai. "Chicago School of Economics Post-Crisis: Interview with John Cassidy." *Marketplace*, January 7, 2010. Accessed January 2, 2016. http://www.marketplace.org/2010/01/07/business/fallout-financial-crisis/chicago-school-economics-post-crisis.

Skousen, Mark, "Who is the Greatest Economist of the Twentieth Century?" Last modified February 5, 1999. http://mskousen.com/1999/02/who-is-the-greatest-economist-of-the-20th-century.

Smith, Adam. *The Theory of Moral Sentiments*. London: A. Millar, 1759.

Solow, Robert M. "Hayek, Friedman, and the Illusions of Conservative Economics." *New Republic*, November 16, 2012. Accessed January 2, 2016. https://newrepublic.com/article/110196/hayek-friedman-and-the-illusions-conservative-economics.

"Why Is There No Milton Friedman Today?" *Econ Journal Watch* 10, no. 2 (2013).

Stern, Andrew. "Financial Crisis Haunts Milton Friedman's Legacy." *Reuters*, October 14, 2008. Accessed January 6, 2016. http://www.reuters.com/article/us-financial-friedman-chicago-idUSTRE49D9EJ20081014.

Stiglitz, Joseph E. *The Price of Inequality*. New York: W. W. Norton & Company, 2012.

"After the Financial Crisis, We Were All Keynesians – But Not For Long Enough." *Guardian*, October 10, 2013. Accessed January 6, 2016. http://www.theguardian.com/business/economics-blog/2013/oct/10/financial-crisis-keynesians-eurozone-recession.

Wolf, Martin. "Keynes Offers Us the Best Way to Think About the Financial Crisis." *Financial Times*, December 23, 2008. Accessed January 7, 2016. http://www.ft.com/cms/s/0/be2dbf2c-d113-11dd-8cc3-000077b07658.html#axzz3yYYVMwNW.

# THE MACAT LIBRARY
# BY DISCIPLINE

The Macat Library By Discipline

## AFRICANA STUDIES

Chinua Achebe's *An Image of Africa: Racism in Conrad's Heart of Darkness*
W. E. B. Du Bois's *The Souls of Black Folk*
Zora Neale Huston's *Characteristics of Negro Expression*
Martin Luther King Jr's *Why We Can't Wait*
Toni Morrison's *Playing in the Dark: Whiteness in the American Literary Imagination*

## ANTHROPOLOGY

Arjun Appadurai's *Modernity at Large: Cultural Dimensions of Globalisation*
Philippe Ariès's *Centuries of Childhood*
Franz Boas's *Race, Language and Culture*
Kim Chan & Renée Mauborgne's *Blue Ocean Strategy*
Jared Diamond's *Guns, Germs & Steel: the Fate of Human Societies*
Jared Diamond's *Collapse: How Societies Choose to Fail or Survive*
E. E. Evans-Pritchard's *Witchcraft, Oracles and Magic Among the Azande*
James Ferguson's *The Anti-Politics Machine*
Clifford Geertz's *The Interpretation of Cultures*
David Graeber's *Debt: the First 5000 Years*
Karen Ho's *Liquidated: An Ethnography of Wall Street*
Geert Hofstede's *Culture's Consequences: Comparing Values, Behaviors, Institutes and Organizations across Nations*
Claude Lévi-Strauss's *Structural Anthropology*
Jay Macleod's *Ain't No Makin' It: Aspirations and Attainment in a Low-Income Neighborhood*
Saba Mahmood's *The Politics of Piety: The Islamic Revival and the Feminist Subjec*t
Marcel Mauss's *The Gift*

## BUSINESS

Jean Lave & Etienne Wenger's *Situated Learning*
Theodore Levitt's *Marketing Myopia*
Burton G. Malkiel's *A Random Walk Down Wall Street*
Douglas McGregor's *The Human Side of Enterprise*
Michael Porter's *Competitive Strategy: Creating and Sustaining Superior Performance*
John Kotter's *Leading Change*
C. K. Prahalad & Gary Hamel's *The Core Competence of the Corporation*

## CRIMINOLOGY

Michelle Alexander's *The New Jim Crow: Mass Incarceration in the Age of Colorblindness*
Michael R. Gottfredson & Travis Hirschi's *A General Theory of Crime*
Richard Herrnstein & Charles A. Murray's *The Bell Curve: Intelligence and Class Structure in American Life*
Elizabeth Loftus's *Eyewitness Testimony*
Jay Macleod's *Ain't No Makin' It: Aspirations and Attainment in a Low-Income Neighborhood*
Philip Zimbardo's *The Lucifer Effect*

## ECONOMICS

Janet Abu-Lughod's *Before European Hegemony*
Ha-Joon Chang's *Kicking Away the Ladder*
David Brion Davis's *The Problem of Slavery in the Age of Revolution*
Milton Friedman's *The Role of Monetary Policy*
Milton Friedman's *Capitalism and Freedom*
David Graeber's *Debt: the First 5000 Years*
Friedrich Hayek's *The Road to Serfdom*
Karen Ho's *Liquidated: An Ethnography of Wall Street*

John Maynard Keynes's *The General Theory of Employment, Interest and Money*
Charles P. Kindleberger's *Manias, Panics and Crashes*
Robert Lucas's *Why Doesn't Capital Flow from Rich to Poor Countries?*
Burton G. Malkiel's *A Random Walk Down Wall Street*
Thomas Robert Malthus's *An Essay on the Principle of Population*
Karl Marx's *Capital*
Thomas Piketty's *Capital in the Twenty-First Century*
Amartya Sen's *Development as Freedom*
Adam Smith's *The Wealth of Nations*
Nassim Nicholas Taleb's *The Black Swan: The Impact of the Highly Improbable*
Amos Tversky's & Daniel Kahneman's *Judgment under Uncertainty: Heuristics and Biases*
Mahbub Ul Haq's *Reflections on Human Development*
Max Weber's *The Protestant Ethic and the Spirit of Capitalism*

### FEMINISM AND GENDER STUDIES

Judith Butler's *Gender Trouble*
Simone De Beauvoir's *The Second Sex*
Michel Foucault's *History of Sexuality*
Betty Friedan's *The Feminine Mystique*
Saba Mahmood's *The Politics of Piety: The Islamic Revival and the Feminist Subject*
Joan Wallach Scott's *Gender and the Politics of History*
Mary Wollstonecraft's *A Vindication of the Rights of Woman*
Virginia Woolf's *A Room of One's Own*

### GEOGRAPHY

The Brundtland Report's *Our Common Future*
Rachel Carson's *Silent Spring*
Charles Darwin's *On the Origin of Species*
James Ferguson's *The Anti-Politics Machine*
Jane Jacobs's *The Death and Life of Great American Cities*
James Lovelock's *Gaia: A New Look at Life on Earth*
Amartya Sen's *Development as Freedom*
Mathis Wackernagel & William Rees's *Our Ecological Footprint*

### HISTORY

Janet Abu-Lughod's *Before European Hegemony*
Benedict Anderson's *Imagined Communities*
Bernard Bailyn's *The Ideological Origins of the American Revolution*
Hanna Batatu's *The Old Social Classes And The Revolutionary Movements Of Iraq*
Christopher Browning's *Ordinary Men: Reserve Police Batallion 101 and the Final Solution in Poland*
Edmund Burke's *Reflections on the Revolution in France*
William Cronon's *Nature's Metropolis: Chicago And The Great West*
Alfred W. Crosby's *The Columbian Exchange*
Hamid Dabashi's *Iran: A People Interrupted*
David Brion Davis's *The Problem of Slavery in the Age of Revolution*
Nathalie Zemon Davis's *The Return of Martin Guerre*
Jared Diamond's *Guns, Germs & Steel: the Fate of Human Societies*
Frank Dikotter's *Mao's Great Famine*
John W Dower's *War Without Mercy: Race And Power In The Pacific War*
W. E. B. Du Bois's *The Souls of Black Folk*
Richard J. Evans's *In Defence of History*
Lucien Febvre's *The Problem of Unbelief in the 16th Century*
Sheila Fitzpatrick's *Everyday Stalinism*

The Macat Library By Discipline

Eric Foner's *Reconstruction: America's Unfinished Revolution, 1863-1877*
Michel Foucault's *Discipline and Punish*
Michel Foucault's *History of Sexuality*
Francis Fukuyama's *The End of History and the Last Man*
John Lewis Gaddis's *We Now Know: Rethinking Cold War History*
Ernest Gellner's *Nations and Nationalism*
Eugene Genovese's *Roll, Jordan, Roll: The World the Slaves Made*
Carlo Ginzburg's *The Night Battles*
Daniel Goldhagen's *Hitler's Willing Executioners*
Jack Goldstone's *Revolution and Rebellion in the Early Modern World*
Antonio Gramsci's *The Prison Notebooks*
Alexander Hamilton, John Jay & James Madison's *The Federalist Papers*
Christopher Hill's *The World Turned Upside Down*
Carole Hillenbrand's *The Crusades: Islamic Perspectives*
Thomas Hobbes's *Leviathan*
Eric Hobsbawm's *The Age Of Revolution*
John A. Hobson's *Imperialism: A Study*
Albert Hourani's *History of the Arab Peoples*
Samuel P. Huntington's *The Clash of Civilizations and the Remaking of World Order*
C. L. R. James's *The Black Jacobins*
Tony Judt's *Postwar: A History of Europe Since 1945*
Ernst Kantorowicz's *The King's Two Bodies: A Study in Medieval Political Theology*
Paul Kennedy's *The Rise and Fall of the Great Powers*
Ian Kershaw's *The "Hitler Myth": Image and Reality in the Third Reich*
John Maynard Keynes's *The General Theory of Employment, Interest and Money*
Charles P. Kindleberger's *Manias, Panics and Crashes*
Martin Luther King Jr's *Why We Can't Wait*
Henry Kissinger's *World Order: Reflections on the Character of Nations and the Course of History*
Thomas Kuhn's *The Structure of Scientific Revolutions*
Georges Lefebvre's *The Coming of the French Revolution*
John Locke's *Two Treatises of Government*
Niccolò Machiavelli's *The Prince*
Thomas Robert Malthus's *An Essay on the Principle of Population*
Mahmood Mamdani's *Citizen and Subject: Contemporary Africa And The Legacy Of Late Colonialism*
Karl Marx's *Capital*
Stanley Milgram's *Obedience to Authority*
John Stuart Mill's *On Liberty*
Thomas Paine's *Common Sense*
Thomas Paine's *Rights of Man*
Geoffrey Parker's *Global Crisis: War, Climate Change and Catastrophe in the Seventeenth Century*
Jonathan Riley-Smith's *The First Crusade and the Idea of Crusading*
Jean-Jacques Rousseau's *The Social Contract*
Joan Wallach Scott's *Gender and the Politics of History*
Theda Skocpol's *States and Social Revolutions*
Adam Smith's *The Wealth of Nations*
Timothy Snyder's *Bloodlands: Europe Between Hitler and Stalin*
Sun Tzu's *The Art of War*
Keith Thomas's *Religion and the Decline of Magic*
Thucydides's *The History of the Peloponnesian War*
Frederick Jackson Turner's *The Significance of the Frontier in American History*
Odd Arne Westad's *The Global Cold War: Third World Interventions And The Making Of Our Times*

## LITERATURE

Chinua Achebe's *An Image of Africa: Racism in Conrad's Heart of Darkness*
Roland Barthes's *Mythologies*
Homi K. Bhabha's *The Location of Culture*
Judith Butler's *Gender Trouble*
Simone De Beauvoir's *The Second Sex*
Ferdinand De Saussure's *Course in General Linguistics*
T. S. Eliot's *The Sacred Wood: Essays on Poetry and Criticism*
Zora Neale Huston's *Characteristics of Negro Expression*
Toni Morrison's *Playing in the Dark: Whiteness in the American Literary Imagination*
Edward Said's *Orientalism*
Gayatri Chakravorty Spivak's *Can the Subaltern Speak?*
Mary Wollstonecraft's *A Vindication of the Rights of Women*
Virginia Woolf's *A Room of One's Own*

## PHILOSOPHY

Elizabeth Anscombe's *Modern Moral Philosophy*
Hannah Arendt's *The Human Condition*
Aristotle's *Metaphysics*
Aristotle's *Nicomachean Ethics*
Edmund Gettier's *Is Justified True Belief Knowledge?*
Georg Wilhelm Friedrich Hegel's *Phenomenology of Spirit*
David Hume's *Dialogues Concerning Natural Religion*
David Hume's *The Enquiry for Human Understanding*
Immanuel Kant's *Religion within the Boundaries of Mere Reason*
Immanuel Kant's *Critique of Pure Reason*
Søren Kierkegaard's *The Sickness Unto Death*
Søren Kierkegaard's *Fear and Trembling*
C. S. Lewis's *The Abolition of Man*
Alasdair MacIntyre's *After Virtue*
Marcus Aurelius's *Meditations*
Friedrich Nietzsche's *On the Genealogy of Morality*
Friedrich Nietzsche's *Beyond Good and Evil*
Plato's *Republic*
Plato's *Symposium*
Jean-Jacques Rousseau's *The Social Contract*
Gilbert Ryle's *The Concept of Mind*
Baruch Spinoza's *Ethics*
Sun Tzu's *The Art of War*
Ludwig Wittgenstein's *Philosophical Investigations*

## POLITICS

Benedict Anderson's *Imagined Communities*
Aristotle's *Politics*
Bernard Bailyn's *The Ideological Origins of the American Revolution*
Edmund Burke's *Reflections on the Revolution in France*
John C. Calhoun's *A Disquisition on Government*
Ha-Joon Chang's *Kicking Away the Ladder*
Hamid Dabashi's *Iran: A People Interrupted*
Hamid Dabashi's *Theology of Discontent: The Ideological Foundation of the Islamic Revolution in Iran*
Robert Dahl's *Democracy and its Critics*
Robert Dahl's *Who Governs?*
David Brion Davis's *The Problem of Slavery in the Age of Revolution*

The Macat Library By Discipline

Alexis De Tocqueville's *Democracy in America*
James Ferguson's *The Anti-Politics Machine*
Frank Dikotter's *Mao's Great Famine*
Sheila Fitzpatrick's *Everyday Stalinism*
Eric Foner's *Reconstruction: America's Unfinished Revolution, 1863-1877*
Milton Friedman's *Capitalism and Freedom*
Francis Fukuyama's *The End of History and the Last Man*
John Lewis Gaddis's *We Now Know: Rethinking Cold War History*
Ernest Gellner's *Nations and Nationalism*
David Graeber's *Debt: the First 5000 Years*
Antonio Gramsci's *The Prison Notebooks*
Alexander Hamilton, John Jay & James Madison's *The Federalist Papers*
Friedrich Hayek's *The Road to Serfdom*
Christopher Hill's *The World Turned Upside Down*
Thomas Hobbes's *Leviathan*
John A. Hobson's *Imperialism: A Study*
Samuel P. Huntington's *The Clash of Civilizations and the Remaking of World Order*
Tony Judt's *Postwar: A History of Europe Since 1945*
David C. Kang's *China Rising: Peace, Power and Order in East Asia*
Paul Kennedy's *The Rise and Fall of Great Powers*
Robert Keohane's *After Hegemony*
Martin Luther King Jr.'s *Why We Can't Wait*
Henry Kissinger's *World Order: Reflections on the Character of Nations and the Course of History*
John Locke's *Two Treatises of Government*
Niccolò Machiavelli's *The Prince*
Thomas Robert Malthus's *An Essay on the Principle of Population*
Mahmood Mamdani's *Citizen and Subject: Contemporary Africa And The Legacy Of Late Colonialism*
Karl Marx's *Capital*
John Stuart Mill's *On Liberty*
John Stuart Mill's *Utilitarianism*
Hans Morgenthau's *Politics Among Nations*
Thomas Paine's *Common Sense*
Thomas Paine's *Rights of Man*
Thomas Piketty's *Capital in the Twenty-First Century*
Robert D. Putman's *Bowling Alone*
John Rawls's *Theory of Justice*
Jean-Jacques Rousseau's *The Social Contract*
Theda Skocpol's *States and Social Revolutions*
Adam Smith's *The Wealth of Nations*
Sun Tzu's *The Art of War*
Henry David Thoreau's *Civil Disobedience*
Thucydides's *The History of the Peloponnesian War*
Kenneth Waltz's *Theory of International Politics*
Max Weber's *Politics as a Vocation*
Odd Arne Westad's *The Global Cold War: Third World Interventions And The Making Of Our Times*

## POSTCOLONIAL STUDIES

Roland Barthes's *Mythologies*
Frantz Fanon's *Black Skin, White Masks*
Homi K. Bhabha's *The Location of Culture*
Gustavo Gutiérrez's *A Theology of Liberation*
Edward Said's *Orientalism*
Gayatri Chakravorty Spivak's *Can the Subaltern Speak?*

## PSYCHOLOGY

Gordon Allport's *The Nature of Prejudice*
Alan Baddeley & Graham Hitch's *Aggression: A Social Learning Analysis*
Albert Bandura's *Aggression: A Social Learning Analysis*
Leon Festinger's *A Theory of Cognitive Dissonance*
Sigmund Freud's *The Interpretation of Dreams*
Betty Friedan's *The Feminine Mystique*
Michael R. Gottfredson  & Travis Hirschi's *A General Theory of Crime*
Eric Hoffer's *The True Believer: Thoughts on the Nature of Mass Movements*
William James's *Principles of Psychology*
Elizabeth Loftus's *Eyewitness Testimony*
A. H. Maslow's *A Theory of Human Motivation*
Stanley Milgram's *Obedience to Authority*
Steven Pinker's *The Better Angels of Our Nature*
Oliver Sacks's *The Man Who Mistook His Wife For a Hat*
Richard Thaler & Cass Sunstein's *Nudge: Improving Decisions About Health, Wealth and Happiness*
Amos Tversky's *Judgment under Uncertainty: Heuristics and Biases*
Philip Zimbardo's *The Lucifer Effect*

## SCIENCE

Rachel Carson's *Silent Spring*
William Cronon's *Nature's Metropolis: Chicago And The Great West*
Alfred W. Crosby's *The Columbian Exchange*
Charles Darwin's *On the Origin of Species*
Richard Dawkin's *The Selfish Gene*
Thomas Kuhn's *The Structure of Scientific Revolutions*
Geoffrey Parker's *Global Crisis: War, Climate Change and Catastrophe in the Seventeenth Century*
Mathis Wackernagel & William Rees's *Our Ecological Footprint*

## SOCIOLOGY

Michelle Alexander's *The New Jim Crow: Mass Incarceration in the Age of Colorblindness*
Gordon Allport's *The Nature of Prejudice*
Albert Bandura's *Aggression: A Social Learning Analysis*
Hanna Batatu's *The Old Social Classes And The Revolutionary Movements Of Iraq*
Ha-Joon Chang's *Kicking Away the Ladder*
W. E. B. Du Bois's *The Souls of Black Folk*
Émile Durkheim's *On Suicide*
Frantz Fanon's *Black Skin, White Masks*
Frantz Fanon's *The Wretched of the Earth*
Eric Foner's *Reconstruction: America's Unfinished Revolution, 1863-1877*
Eugene Genovese's *Roll, Jordan, Roll: The World the Slaves Made*
Jack Goldstone's *Revolution and Rebellion in the Early Modern World*
Antonio Gramsci's *The Prison Notebooks*
Richard Herrnstein & Charles A Murray's *The Bell Curve: Intelligence and Class Structure in American Life*
Eric Hoffer's *The True Believer: Thoughts on the Nature of Mass Movements*
Jane Jacobs's *The Death and Life of Great American Cities*
Robert Lucas's *Why Doesn't Capital Flow from Rich to Poor Countries?*
Jay Macleod's *Ain't No Makin' It: Aspirations and Attainment in a Low Income Neighborhood*
Elaine May's *Homeward Bound: American Families in the Cold War Era*
Douglas McGregor's *The Human Side of Enterprise*
C. Wright Mills's *The Sociological Imagination*

The Macat Library By Discipline

Thomas Piketty's *Capital in the Twenty-First Century*
Robert D. Putman's *Bowling Alone*
David Riesman's *The Lonely Crowd: A Study of the Changing American Character*
Edward Said's *Orientalism*
Joan Wallach Scott's *Gender and the Politics of History*
Theda Skocpol's *States and Social Revolutions*
Max Weber's *The Protestant Ethic and the Spirit of Capitalism*

### THEOLOGY

Augustine's *Confessions*
Benedict's *Rule of St Benedict*
Gustavo Gutiérrez's *A Theology of Liberation*
Carole Hillenbrand's *The Crusades: Islamic Perspectives*
David Hume's *Dialogues Concerning Natural Religion*
Immanuel Kant's *Religion within the Boundaries of Mere Reason*
Ernst Kantorowicz's *The King's Two Bodies: A Study in Medieval Political Theology*
Søren Kierkegaard's *The Sickness Unto Death*
C. S. Lewis's *The Abolition of Man*
Saba Mahmood's *The Politics of Piety: The Islamic Revival and the Feminist Subject*
Baruch Spinoza's *Ethics*
Keith Thomas's *Religion and the Decline of Magic*

### COMING SOON

Chris Argyris's *The Individual and the Organisation*
Seyla Benhabib's *The Rights of Others*
Walter Benjamin's *The Work Of Art in the Age of Mechanical Reproduction*
John Berger's *Ways of Seeing*
Pierre Bourdieu's *Outline of a Theory of Practice*
Mary Douglas's *Purity and Danger*
Roland Dworkin's *Taking Rights Seriously*
James G. March's *Exploration and Exploitation in Organisational Learning*
Ikujiro Nonaka's *A Dynamic Theory of Organizational Knowledge Creation*
Griselda Pollock's *Vision and Difference*
Amartya Sen's *Inequality Re-Examined*
Susan Sontag's *On Photography*
Yasser Tabbaa's *The Transformation of Islamic Art*
Ludwig von Mises's *Theory of Money and Credit*

# Macat Disciplines

*Access the greatest ideas and thinkers across entire disciplines, including*

## *Postcolonial Studies*

**Roland Barthes's** *Mythologies*
**Frantz Fanon's** *Black Skin, White Masks*
**Homi K. Bhabha's** *The Location of Culture*
**Gustavo Gutiérrez's** *A Theology of Liberation*
**Edward Said's** *Orientalism*
**Gayatri Chakravorty Spivak's** *Can the Subaltern Speak?*

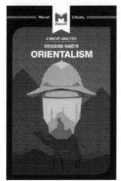

Macat analyses are available from all good bookshops and libraries.

Access hundreds of analyses through one, multimedia tool.

Join free for one month **library.macat.com**

Printed in the United States
by Baker & Taylor Publisher Services